The Emotions Anthology Box Set

Emotions

in

Eruption
Evolution
Existence

Barbara Strickland

Copyright © 2019 Barbara Strickland

www.brstrickland.com

Barbara Strickland asserts the moral right to be identified as the author of this work.

All rights reserved

No part of this book may be reproduced or transmitted in any form or by any means, electronic or mechanical, including photocopying, recording or any information storage and retrieval system, without prior permission in writing from the author, nor be otherwise circulated in any form of binding or cover other than that in which it is published and without a similar condition including this condition being imposed on the subsequent purchaser. Brief quotations embodied in critical articles or reviews are permitted.

The names, characters and events portrayed in this publication other than those clearly in the public domain, are fictitious and the work of the author's imagination. Any resemblance to real persons, living or dead is purely coincidental.

Emotions Erupting, Evolving and Existing Copyright © 2019

Emotions in Existence Copyright © 2019

Emotions in Evolution Copyright © 2018 Barbara Strickland

Emotions in Eruption Copyright © 2018 Barbara Strickland (2017)

Extract from Unexpected Obsession Copyright © 2017 Barbara Strickland (2016)

Extract from Unexpected Passion "Unpublished Work © 2019 Barbara Strickland"

Extract from The Narrow Hallway "Unpublished Work © 2019 Barbara Strickland"

Author's note: This book was written in Australia and uses British/Australian spelling conventions such as 'colour' instead of 'color', and 'ise' endings instead of 'ize' on words like 'realize'. Some words will also have double ll in its spelling e.g. travel will become travelling.

Cover designs and illustrations by Christopher Brunton

http://www.cjbrunton.wix.com/brunton-illustration

DEDICATION

For my son Daniel on his 40th Birthday

I don't have much to give in monetary value, but I think I was gifted a small talent, and the ability to believe nothing is impossible. This is the culmination of a project I have worked towards hoping I would reach the end, but not quite sure I could.

Keeping the belief alive is hard work as you get older but sometimes you say things to me, and I am reminded of who I am, and it inspires me to fight harder to continue to work towards that impossible.

Happy Birthday, I love you and am so proud of the way you tackle that impossible, and so incredibly happy that you do it so much better than me.

Acknowledgements

Writing and what is involved is difficult and keeping confidence intact often seems impossible. People keep you going, and they deserve acknowledgement. Thank you to my dear friend Trish who reads what I write and adds a grammatical touch when I forget to. I couldn't do without your endless rounds of reading and checking. Thank you to Julia for being like another daughter and a sounding board all in one. I'd adopt you if I could. Melanie, you have become family and you listen, and you are loved whether you live here or overseas. Sue, I just plain loved you from the first moment we met at University.

Luke, you have been incredibly encouraging and helpful, and Sean and Kathy, Kaye and Alyson, you were there at the start and hold my heart. Kirsty, your kindness blows me away. To my list of great people, I add Jill, a late friendship but such a positive one, and Gavin, a very talented writer, poet and artist, and my mentor in the Japanese poetry. Last but far from least my warmest regards to a group of incredible authors, artists, poets and readers I have met while navigating my way with social media over this last year. The support has been phenomenal. Writing may be a solitary profession but achieving in any measure occurs because whilst our work may be solitary, our lives are not.

Thank you to my family, Tara, your support and trust are beyond words. I am blessed with wonderful children, their spouses and grandchildren. It all helps. A special mention to my cousin Rita who has kept me buoyant with phone calls, a sense of humour and affection.

In loving memory

To Rose and Vince (my parents),

I wish I had your poems to translate Rose, but
reading your writing was impossible. I hope you can
settle for passing on the love of poetry. Your
scribblings, Vince, were constant, and so are mine.
My love for education came from you.
Share this with me, it's the best I can do.

To my dearest friend Gail.

I carry the memory of your courage in my heart. You are
now with someone who will love you and keep you, safe
forever. I will miss you always.
Thank you for being my friend,
Barb
(Don't worry, Norfolk is on, give me a little more time
and I will figure it out)

Table of Contents

Emotions in Eruption

(1)

Emotions in Evolution

(126)

Emotions in Existence

(260)

From the Author

(1 - 76)

Emotions in Eruption

A poetic journey through life

Barbara Strickland

Foreword Emotions in Eruption (8)

REFLECTIONS (10)

Easy Listening (11)

On Thinking Too Much (13)

Lost Art of Friendship (15)

Decision Making (17)

The Buds (19)

HUMAN CONTACT (20)

Nobody Is Perfect (I love you) (21)

Birthing (23)

Butterfly Child (25)

Binary Opposition (27)

Players (29)

Distractions of the Heart (31)

Lucid Tranquillity (33)

The Cabbage Patch Doll (36)

REALITY (37)

Forgotten Magic (38)

Spring Blossoms (39)

Choosing Blindness (40)

Competition (42)

Imagine (44)

Dreaming (46)

The Stubborn Heart (48)

Romantic Fantasy (49)

Don't Shut the Door (50)

The Dreamer Never Dies (52)

Semantics (54)

A Simply Stunning Slaughter (55)

The Extension (57)

Soul-Kissed (Nico's Lament) (59)

Ignorance (61)

SORROW (63)

Self-Portrait (64)

Night and Day (65)

Anorexic Purging (66)

Impossible Lover (Nico's Ode to Lia) (67)

Invisible (69)

Depressed – To Be or Not To Be (71)

Addictive Patterns (73)

Self-Harm (75)

Sad Movies Make Me Cry (77)

This Last Episode (79)

The Waiting Game (81)

Desert Living (83)

Broken Promises (85)

Monsoonal Madness (87)

Petulance (89)

Immobilisation (90)

Deprivation (92)

Desperation (94)

CROSSROADS (96)

Oops, I Messed Up Again (97)

I Am Not in Love (99)

Intersection (101)

Midnight Deception (103)

Indifference (104)

Adulthood (106)

Change of Life (108)

Missing the Boat (110)

NEXT (112)

Seasons in Turmoil (113)

Belonging (115)

At the End (117)

PEOPLE AND WINE (119)

People are like fine wine (120)

The Adventurer (121)

The Pacifist (121)

The Sensualist (122)

The Pleasure Seeker (122)

The Thinker (123)

The Conversationalist (123)

CHERRY BLOSSOMS (124)

Haiku Memories (124)

Foreword to Emotions in Eruption

Putting pen to paper, or rather fingers to a keyboard can be quite confronting. Automatically there is a suggestion that the words matter. They do. Your words should matter. Words lend strength and give voice. Silence holds us back.

I wrote this because in times of crisis I give myself a voice. At times that voice may seem exaggerated, emotional, a little bizarre, or left field but it is real. It exists. I cope by putting and yes at times *over putting* (over sharing perhaps) things down on paper. I have been lost, lonely and unhappy. I have been delighted, dazzled and elated. It is the nature of the world and its people to feel emotions, both good and bad.

However, when the feelings are not pleasant the tendency is to hide, to believe we are alone and foolish in our thoughts and reactions. For me sharing in the form of writing, any kind, helps me find perspective. We are supposed to hide the negative and thus feel guilty because in sharing we believe we burden. I disagree. By speaking we face our fears, and if we are fortunate, we find understanding. In speaking up we are seeking a solution. We burden when we hide. That battle fatigues our soul.

Sometimes the instinct to survive is shrouded in semantics, both for speaker and the hearer of the language for though love is supposed to be unconditional, the reality of life intrudes. The expectancy is to be strong, to be positive and to perform accordingly. In theory it sounds good and I wish it was possible to obliterate negative thoughts and actions. It's not. It is the contrariness of human beings.

The price is a fragile butterfly that emerges and doesn't know how to fit into the limitations on offer. Without a leaf of light on which to rest the butterfly will falter and the delicate flavour of finely spun wings will dissipate into the breeze and be gone. We need to be exactly who we are, and not someone others believe we should be, or we risk becoming a creature folding its wings and becoming an unseen whisper.

But words can bring us freedom from pain and unfold the wings to fly again another day. I would have perished without my ability to express my thoughts. I don't need any one to approve them or to like how they appear on the page, but my hope is one word resonates and then someone out there knows they are not alone.
Barbara Strickland

Don't hurt the butterfly, it will die soon enough

Reflections

Do you see only what you think is there?

Easy Listening

*I remember when it was all laid out
what role to take.
You want to shout
it was simple.*

*Waiting to be told
what clothes, what food, when, where
because otherwise was bold.
It was simple.*

*Directed how to achieve
grasping for prizes was controlled
but easy if you wanted to believe –
it was simple.*

*Life demands choices,
cryptic variants of
different paths and loud voices
searching for what is simple.*

Longing deep for normality,

the memories seem safe.
Age brings a strange formality
asking was simple ever there?

On Thinking Too Much

How to make it stop
so that it recedes, disappears,
this constant turning of thoughts
that haunt me, even in
those precious moments
when joy, exists?
I did not want to feel.
I was right. But, the
need to take a chance
was stronger than
I expected and so I entered
that frightening world.
No peace there because
I was right.
And now pain pierces painfully.
I am scarred, bruised and
lonely when before I was
just alone.

I was wrong to believe in

fairy tales, and white horses, and

handsome heroes.

Now with cold certainty

I must learn to forget

how to read.

Lost Art of Friendship

Ethereal magic.
Substantial.
A butterfly kiss,
so light, that
even to breathe
becomes a dare.
Warmth, spreading and
touching my often cold,
and always bleeding heart.
Overwhelming,
so that at the fall
of darkness there is
an abundance of light
to relinquish the ever
present pain beyond
my elusive control.
Are you real?
Are you a dream sequence?

16

Is that your

voice, or my mind?

Whatever, whoever,

you are the living

proof of the meeting

of souls.

You are my friend

when I take the time

to see you.

Decision Making

I don't want to.

Instead

I feel the urge to

rant and rave.

I know I have to.

Instead

I feel the urge to

quietly cave.

I've been dealt a card.

It's far too hard.

I close my eyes

and hope

I wake up wise.

I have seen the

echoed smile reflected,

in a happiness file.

I carefully remove

18

all the shiny blades,

sighing as the

anger fades.

The Buds

Rustling winds call my name

and awaken me to play the game.

I slowly dress

and to myself confess

though the rules seem less,

nothing seems the same.

Whirling wheels of distant blame

reluctantly decide to claim

the fading lights

of long-lost flights,

and unwanted plights

leading back to covert shame.

To the recesses of yesterday

I banish all dead flowers.

Let them rest where they may

and allow new buds their untried powers.

Human Contact

Pieces on boards are moved by humans.

Nobody is Perfect (I love you)

Often, I wonder why
you have the power
to make cry.
The sudden silence of my heart
understands,
knows, all
you do is simply thoughtless.
Sometimes fine,
sometimes cold
and cruel
so that an oozing occurs.
There is bleeding as
the sharp knife, you plunge.
The deep and sudden penetration
is bitter and I find it
hard to remember that
I wanted and needed you.
Never did I dream

that this kind of love could

be a torment.

In growing up

the distance must have shifted.

Whereas before your childhood needs

tore at my core,

I find now you rip me

into shreds,

and I have not the energy

to repair the threads.

Yet I am amazed at what you can do.

That glimpsed rich smile

directed my way,

has so much power

to make me say,

it does not matter those things

I filed,

for after all you are

and always will be

my beloved born child.

Birthing

A small vibration builds

slowly, piercingly pinching

and penetrating like a summer insect

that at dusk must come out

to show the night as an

imperfect medium contrasting

with bitingly bitter stinging sensations

to the sweetness of the sun filled days.

A constant running of close

together eruptions, erosions

and errors of nature which

display a natural process as an

imperfect medium contrasting

the truisms handed down since the

beginning of time and human evolution.

A final cutting edge of sans pity

statements screaming sinfully silent

and showing only at the

almost merciless end

that the imperfect medium is

in contrast to

what you imagined

a long yearned for

and deeply desired creation.

Butterfly Child (Lia's song)

Because of you

I feel the lightest touch of soft satin wings.

I see the rainbow in all things.

If I could contain you upon my hand,

you would be as delicate as grains of sand.

Finely formed, reflecting the glimmer of summer shine,

sweet of temper and pure of soul,

such a strong straight line.

You are the best of me.

You are the gift only of

the Butterfly that I am and so

you are the softness of my wings, and

the rainbow colours that I wear I

bequeath to you because in

you they flourish.

And

so, I think it only fair to for you to know

when I am long gone from you and

you see a butterfly passing by,

it will be me that you do not see

and it will be me reminding you, that

every day in every way

I loved you more

than I knew to say.

Binary Opposition

We were a union made to explore.

One heartbeat,

strong and sure.

A physicality to be admired,

a truth of mind and core.

One of us dissipated,

melted, dissolved but essence

remained to taunt that one of us

left alone to

inhabit that secret place.

Made to stay there,

alone, afraid

and in the dark,

ignored, and deplored I

hoped to escape your mark.

Shuddering, I accepted you were

ingrained. You colour my blood.

You are the language that explains me

and you have the right not

to be starved by my frightened soul.

Come, take your light.

Join me now

for we are meant to be

and this time I will allow

your Growth, and I will

not call your goodness weak.

And I will

not be afraid to love

completely, unconditionally

with all that I am

for I am tired

and can no longer

play the game

on this broken stage

by myself.

Players

Chance meeting.

Pleasant, nice,

but safety rules.

Pieces are moved forward.

Silent pawns stand unafraid.

This is only an interlude.

Sudden tension.

Fearful, unbearable.

The Queen is in check.

She remains unthreatened

but knows the game has changed.

There is need for reflection.

The King glides forward,

demanding, powerfully intent.

The Queen is aloof.

Uncertainty brings sacrifices

and

the board is now alien.

The precipice is jagged.

She alone must decide.

She alone moves forward.

Danger pervades but

the prize is golden, attainable

and

worth the risk.

This is more than an interlude.

The King senses capitulation.

The King moves.

The King purposefully turns.

The King is not ready for veracity.

He moves away callously.

The Queen dies.

Distractions of the Heart

Abandonment of all those dreams,

concentration instead on schemes.

Forget the longing and heart-felt yearning,

the future beckons and the wheels are turning.

But I whisper to the wind distracted,

maybe this time I will not be compacted.

Liar, Liar, inside your mind you shout,

this is not the end of the drought.

You are hoping,

you are moping,

you are not ready for another coping.

This time it will be different,

you are not swimming against the current.

You came to this with some insight.

You fought a brave and gallant fight.

But I whisper to the wind in sweet rapture,

will loving slowly, prevent the fracture?

Liar, Liar, inside your mind you shout.

Do not go there and forget to doubt.

You are running.

He is cunning.

You are not ready for another gunning.

What do I do then with this distraction?

Do I turn away from the attraction?

And so, I do my whispering to the wind,

and hope with all my heart

this time, he will not rescind.

I am a fool to make this admission.

I cannot help myself; I want remission.

Lucid Tranquillity

I hear You.

But, those voices,

those escalating influences

call me and I falter.

Your echo is far better.

It triggers a spiritual spiral

towards a lucidity

so often escaping my notice.

To be calm,

to be tranquil shudders

me into splintered fragile

snowflakes of melting

emotional madness.

I know I am the creator.

I know my power but

still I am hostage to

silvered slides of

syntax makers, who want

their universal limitations

to rule supreme

over others, others

who do not understand

the glory of manifestation

and sadly, cowardly

bend to the collector.

I am left frozen,

the withered wraith

of a broken spirit

bereft of presence,

a diminished aura

of splattered, faded and

crumbling colours

never to blend.

I hear You.

I know what You say.

Be patience generous,

for I am

only now unfurling

from

my embryonic

prison.

The Cabbage Patch Doll

I saw it first as small

and sweet.

I saw it then get

on its feet.

Giant steps, giant words.

The doll-like creature

had an adult-like feature.

I cried and cried

and thought I'd died.

Giant steps, giant words,

until the human hands

back from foreign lands

opened up, to reveal,

what suddenly I could feel.

The cabbage patch now was full.

I let myself enjoy the pull.

Now I watch the dolls at play

and happily, keep the tears at bay.

Reality

We begin, we end. We can only hope the in-between is not left blank.

Forgotten Magic

In the music of your silence

comes the perfect peace as

green and grasping you

touch my soul with your

magical root-centred existence.

The darkness you inhabit

is dense and full-bodied, holding

fears in perspective, for

underneath hungrily avid is

Life in rainbow-coloured glory.

I may never get the

chance to see your

undoubted splendour, for I live

ensnared by different choices.

Nevertheless,

I hope.

Spring Blossoms

*Pretty blossoms to be
adored with pleasure.
Drawn, pulled from the deepest
part of the earth to grow,
to prove beauty is really
from within. For are not
the trunk and branches ugly in the
winter frozen chill?*

*Delicate, the softest of colour
combinations, barely there
and yet such a bold fashion
statement to represent the coming of
a new season,
and a new beginning.
I wish we could
be so
simply beautiful.*

Choosing Blindness

The music flows.

Sometimes smooth,

an uninterrupted path

into the soul.

Generous acceptance may allow

completed entry, to make the whole.

Fearful hesitancy, unspoken barriers,

control graceful gratitude

and destroy the magic

of the pleasant interlude.

The loser moves silently along

severely clever, not glimpsing joy.

Value lost, ignored, unseen, and

agonizingly, a deflected ploy.

Did you know, during that endless search,

you alone held the key?
The music will always flow
but not for you, afraid to know.

Competition

In the marketplace of

sheer commodity

you wonder fiercely

about your oddity.

Exclusivity is your sole aim.

But the playing board denotes

a violent game.

Questions fly with deadly speed.

Voracity must rise to meet the need.

You cry choose me, choose me

and have no patience then

to wait and see, and

life revolves around the passion

that kills, destroys and

mutilates compassion.

You need to stay alert to read the news.

You must be on top to get the clues.

Those paradigms are flying fast

and you need to be the first, not last.

Open eyes and listen well.

Prepare to run upon the bell.

Imagine

Peaceful thoughts and

an ability to get through the

Day and Night without the

constant distraction of buts

and dreaded ifs and maybes

of the so-called normal life.

We search the world.

We search new things

to do and make and

we look for hobbies,

we try the different.

We change the people

in our lives

and still we cannot find.

It is somewhere out there

eluding us, taunting us and we

weep. We let anger rule

and frustration reign

when all the time

it is right here.

It is not the geography

that gives us tranquillity

but rather the acceptance of

ourselves.

Dreaming

If I could manifest my thoughts

to you

upon the breeze they would float

and sit

until you allowed that moment

when

absorption occurs, and they melt

inside your mind.

You would take them with a

puzzled distraught frown,

your internals turning, churning,

thrashing up and down

and you would know deep in

that silent waiting part

that it is a waste of time

to be so mindlessly far apart.

But this is reality, a test of faith and give.

And right this minute, you are far too human,

to let my manifestations in

and let them live.

I will wait, I know you.

You will come to me.

I have waited this long,

I will wait a little bit longer

for where I belong.

The Stubborn Heart

Every time I allow my heart
to open like the proverbial door
I also choose a poison dart
and engage in hurt a little more.

It's time to stop not start
to protect that tiny internal core.
Acknowledgement in blood
must be minimal
to prevent that dreaded flood.
Sad cannot be subliminal.

Black, iron cast impenetrable door
Where heavy handles block my power
The heart rules less, the head rules more
And my face becomes dismally and forever dour.

Romantic Fantasy

One look and it seems

enough.

One touch and the magician

lives.

No doubts,

no insecurities.

Joy reigns.

Bubbling infectious domino

effect.

My pillows hit the wooden floor.

My mobile calls my name.

Ha! I was dreaming.

What a damned shame!

Don't Shut the Door

I tried so hard.

I tried so long.

I turned each card.

I heard each song.

Every single time

I sought the rhyme.

You know the one.

It begins the fun.

I ran towards the road

breaking every traffic code.

I ran towards the church steeple

praying for less elusive people.

I ran back home,

too tired now to roam,

too many answers yet to find,

too many faces so unkind.

I still had hope

and the ability to cope

until I slammed

into the door.

You know the one.

It lands you on the

floor

and stops the fun.

The Dreamer Never Dies

Again, I listen.
Again, I am a prisoner
of that cunning heart
that refuses time and time again
to stop believing in those
dreadful fairy tales
that reek of love and romance
and goodness and happy endings.
Traitor, I call that beating organ
that has no ability to
stop and think what it will
mean to bleed. For God's sake the
fool forgets it is a main
supply of life force and
to bleed once more will evaporate
the last vestige of hope,
a vampire death where I walk
but my life is empty.

It was the music.

It drew out possibilities I had

long ago put in a box.

I really should stop playing the music.

Semantics

Solitary is being alone.

Different to

being lonely.

Alone is a choosing to be.

Confusion so often becomes

interchangeable and so we move

between two worlds, always afraid

to know the consequences, and

making choices from avoidance until

reality comes your way

in silken softness you

cruelly dissect, and the pieces stay

in your heart and your soul

and you drown

and you become lonelier.

Alone is so much better.

A Simply Stunning Slaughter

Breathe gently, move slowly.
The floor below is fragile glass.
Smile, drift and freely float
and let the music dancing, entice.

The mice are handsome.
The pumpkin is rich and golden.
Your clothing bold and daring
and your slippers concreted to the ground.

Enjoy the magical world appearing,
and be radiantly enmeshed in moonlight.
You are the soft sensation of a cloud.
You are the warming hearth where dreams exist.

Defenceless then,
you become the hopeless victim to
the never imagined, simply stunning

slaughter of your mind.

The Extension

I listen for the sound.

I wait for that light,

to flash blood.

I have to answer, now

before

it all becomes a flood.

A finger takes it to

Person A,

another one becomes

Person B.

Each time, exciting and new,

not

that I ever see.

My life is a reflection.

I live

in the in-between.

I hear everything but

I live,

where I can't

be seen.

The solid black gets

human contact.

It survives to feel

the grasp of fingers,

the touch of skin.

Should I envy

that unliving being?

Yes, of course.

It has no ability to sin.

***Soul-Kissed** (Nico's Lament)*

Awareness so profound

I tremble when you are around.

Adaption so intense

that my intelligence makes no sense.

You live inside my head.

You will live until I am dead.

Chemistry is just a word

to minimise what has occurred.

I bent and kissed your mouth

and to my heart your taste went south.

It fooled me into thinking

love would not cloud my sinking.

I thought I could just stimulate

returning later to manipulate.

Selfishness drove my need

as my ego fought to feed.

What we got was so much more

than I ever dreamed to explore.
I think on reflection we soul kissed.
Fearfully I brutally dismissed.
Then I discovered I was blind
for soul-kissers cannot unbind.
We are forever forged and fused
and those who watch are well amused.
I thought I played a mortal game
with courage then to take the blame.
But when you soul-kiss you become a fool
and fall into that deep and endless pool
where no escape will let you free
where no peace will ever be
for you must pay with deep regret.
Soul-kissing is not something you can forget.

Ignorance

Visions

constantly

turning over

so that the mind

never sleeps.

Where, why,

what purpose?

Admit and acknowledge

justifications that the

insecurity of the reality in

comparison to comfort is

only a perception.

Interpretations

so constant they

become a bible.

A religion then

*so deeply ingrained
it becomes disdain,
contempt, and
a critique of all
outside limits of the
narrow globe we live in.*

*Warmth, disappearing.
Frigidity settling in and
creating divisions. Spheres
becoming smaller,
disintegrating
into waxen dust.
Plastic missing
the vital irritation
cannot be ignored.
A death of the soul is
he who is there
with no one to care.*

Sorrow

Sadness is just a state of mind. Change it.

Self-Portrait

*Intricate patterns of clear
interwoven with butterflies and
tulips, the stain of reality for
the mind, represented.
Colours, beautiful, bold
and catching the sight but
not the eye for
the eye will recognise fragility
but sight will see stained glass.
Delicate, easily shattered.
Fragmented into the mixed
tiny, shiny pieces that can be
subtly shaped to appear
meaningful, but are in truth
deceptively inclined to
hide what is after all
damaged goods and broken glass,
no matter the fixation of Glory.*

Night and Day

I love you.

I fear you.

When I am there,

you are here.

When I am here

you disappear.

An illusion

to soul give?

In forever,

can I believe?

There is light

and then darkness

when you leave

my side and I discover,

the deepest part of me you

sever.

Anorexic Purging

Mindless chasing of rainbows
putting true existence in doubt.
But, does not reality reign ruthless and
often at the cost of clarity?
Is this the only way?
Desperate alienation
of soul, and mind?
Where is inner peace?
I hunger for it and
throw it back. I feed
and cannot be fed.
I starve myself with greed.
I purge, I eat, I purge
but never does the balance
I seek show itself.
There is nothing of me
but human, unsightly flesh.
I hate it. Make it disappear.

Impossible Lover (Nico's Ode to Lia)

Fragile in your

steel frame.

Surprisingly passionate,

so unexpected, so intense,

so boundless and

God forgive me

so vulnerable.

Intelligent in your

eggshell abode.

Surprisingly addictive,

so true, so vital,

so focused and

God forgive me

so ill chosen.

A loving heart,

in this heartless world.

I am forever

remorseful.

Life toyed, played a confusingly cruel and disenchanting game.

Invisible

Mine is,

a loneliness

of the soul.

Part of, and

apart from,

I move in the reality

of dreams

where everything is

not what it seems.

Fragmented,

mosaic.

A puzzle within a

puzzle, the

scattered pieces of

life move into

irrational gleams

of somewhat distant

unsynchronized scenes.
My choice,
based on my perceived
needs and desire to
fight the unearthly fire.

Destructive,
cleansing extremities
of my nature.
Fragmented mosaic
tiles of history
denied existence
with ego selfishness.
In sleep perhaps
a union of small pieces
where everything is
just what it seems.

Depressed – To Be or Not To Be

Distanced from the

Detail overview.

Deceptively quiet inside.

Deadly loud outside.

Do get out of bed.

Do not break this stillness.

Directions from the head,

Distractions from the heart.

Duty is calling.

Death calls louder.

Decisions

Distress

Dignity is pretence.

Disaster is reality.

Do pull yourself together.

Do enter the pain realm.

Diligence

Digression

Do I want to be good?

Do I have the energy?

Do I want answers?

Do I know the questions?

Depression

Do I start the process?

Does the process start me?

Do I care?

I need to stop and think.

Addictive Patterns

*Desires circle in the
mind,
that void of brainless
thought,
never learning until
the ending is confused
and the starting line
is never crossed.*

*Days cycling by like
metres
and metres of environmental
sameness,
never ending until
the beginning is confused
and the finishing line
is never reached.*

Fragile heart now,

Pieces of glass.

Splintered.

Shattered

and thrown in

so many directions

that the home is

displaced and

both beginning and ending

have co-inhabited

and

there is no place to go.

No beginning – you no longer dare.

No ending – you were never there.

Self-Harm

I just tried again.

Don't bother with towels or cloths.

There was no blood.

unless you count the

liquid spillage that

tears bring even if

they are dry-eyed delivered.

It was far more, subtle,

more personal,

more painful and severely unseen.

Unless of course there

were witnesses to see.

You believe in Him,

The Being above,

Who knows all,

Who watches helpless but

with desperate hope,

desperate belief, and

desperate hard-won faith

and you finally ask

the question.

Is this the last time?

It wasn't. It isn't.

Sad Movies Make Me Cry

Cold and calculating.

My God, that is fascinating.

Ambivalent, or belligerent?

How exciting? How very different?

Time to laugh, time to smile,

emotions coming out file by file.

Dear, that is so very bad.

I think that character is quite mad.

Please do not let him die.

Oh goodness me, what a terrible lie.

They have come so far. Do they have to part?

So much to sacrifice,

for the sake of Art?

Sad movies make me cry.

Reality only makes me sigh.

Sad movies make me feel

and forget the real.

Sad movies fade away, but

life is here.

Every single day.

I think that I will leave

the TV on

even if others

frown upon

the box where I behold

the watching of the world, unfold.

I would rather watch than participate.

I would rather watch than activate.

This Last Episode

Not the last be sure
but this one, effectively chilling
dampening the glow of
soul-reached compromise
and bringing back the
battle-fixed arena where
fear is constant and
trust the fearful enemy.

Amazing behaviour.
Unnecessary, taunting, painful
when belief in magic
is much sweeter.
But, and but is forcefully
if frantically in existence, the
true sorrow is found to have
shifted from you, yourself,
to them, themselves, who

live without the vestige of

delicious hope within.

Fools! It transcends

what is,

to what may still be.

The Waiting Game

A somewhat intricate beauty

fills my vision and

it disturbs my tired body.

The scene blurs, merges

becoming distorted between the

world that is and the world

I want it to be.

I long for the

carousel to stop.

It is internal and

relentless in its turning.

It prods, pulls and punishes.

It questions, raises doubts.

The destination is unknown

and beyond the knowledge

of the me that has

become the me,

that is the now.

I see it clearly.
That resting place
I long have searched,
and know it is real,
know it exists.
Have I been there
and missed it all?
What is imagination?
What is need?
What is longing?
What is real?
It is my Carousel.

I press the button.

Desert Living

I hate the way nobody sees,

nobody listens.

Eyes are for viewing,

taking in the tiny drops of

life

revolving,

evolving,

and happening

constantly around us

except in this silent

wasteland of nothingness

where a crowded visual is

a stretch of

empty sand.

Ears are for hearing

the sounds that

rustle, slowly feeding

awareness of

life

revolving.

evolving,

and happening

constantly around us,

except in this busy

expansion of nothingness

where a noisy wind is

an expanse of

empty clouds.

Why so blind?
Why so deaf?
I am desperate.
I dehydrate
a little more each day.

Broken Promises

Trappings of gold and white

inhabiting four walls,

sharing surface things until

you wonder what is real

and

what is not,

what is enough

and

what is social illusion

and

dictionary definition

totally out of context

with satin sheets

and lonely nights

even when

a breath away.

And,

a lifetime goes by

and

you are still waiting

to

have it made clear

but

the book is jargonised,

a dichotomy of rules

and

you are language-less

enough already

with

all you have so naively given.

And,

you wake up

and

finally, thankfully,

you are living by yourself,

alone.

Monsoonal Madness

A drop. A drop.

A tiny little drop.

It went away.

It had nothing

whatever to say.

When it came again,

it was barely there

but some heard

despite pitifully

whispered sounds.

Later some called it

a bombardment

of strange ideas

and burning tears.

It left for unknown places.

It was only, drops of water.

Why then did it feel like slaughter,

a mindless destruction

of pitiful faces?

Petulance

What is it?
A mind thing or
the invisible wound on
the abstract heart that
foolishly allows entry.

What does it do?
Travels insidiously in
the veins of emotions to
mark territory signs at
the deepest root base.

Who does it?
You! And all those
others who savagely
partake in the ego dubious
thrill
of soul demise.

Immobilisation

I have seen the Light
but I feel cold.
I have seen the Dark
but I am far too warm
to find comfort
or peace.

Immobile to move forward
and unable to go back
I have found a purgatory of
day-to-day existence.
It is not living.
It is immobilising.

Momentary joys are followed
by the hollowness of
confusion.
Where do we find the wheels?

Where are my roller blades?
Where is my vehicle of escape?

This path is hazardous.
The road is badly concreted
and full of holes, tumours, dark
and pitted and when it ends
I find the familiar pattern
inside my head.

Navigation is possible.
Maps are found
in plentiful array.
Diagrams help plot
the path. Unfortunately
I am immobile by choice.

Deprivation

Can this continue?

This lack of breath,

this frozen state?

Yet it does.

And days go by

and no one and nothing

notices blood in the snow.

It hurts the most

what others miss.

A black hole of tears

never cried because

the Abyss is huge

and the pain voracious

and there is no way to demand

attention because the oxygen is almost gone.

I can't breathe in

and I am afraid to breathe out

and I don't know what is in-between.

The process of life is missing

and despite the savage suction of sound

there is only silence to hear me.

Desperation

Does no-one care

about

loneliness and despair?

I am fading into the night

lacking memories of the light.

Cold, the icicles form around me,

a door without a key.

They stand silent witnesses

as I mourn, sad,

frightenedly forlorn.

I feel buried.

I am trapped.

All my energy has been sapped.

The hurt has changed to deadly.

It has become bitterness friendly.

I am now afraid of the dark.

I can't rid myself of its mark.

I know if I try,

I can switch on that light.

What if I prefer to die

to escape this confusing,

overwhelming,

painful,

insight?

Crossroads

I don't know which path to take. Do you?

Oops, I Messed Up Again

Today I fell and
turned back time.
Pushing, battling to
move on, I tired. And,
yearned for mediocrity.

The past pulls tightly
at the subconscious mind.
It has already failed to
move on because
it knows only mediocrity.

The penalty of femaleness,
to fear the independence of
aloneness.
My heart breaking,
my will forsaking,
my body shaking

with determination,

I try to stand up.

The floor is slippery.

A change of shoes may be in order.

I Am Not in Love

Inexplicable, to feel this way

when the mind is

screaming rationalise,

conclude, then exclude.

This obsession that is now

a point of no return and

a cause to bleed until

even the most ravenous of

vampire is bloated and

ready for true death, forsaking

the pretence of living that

is excitement only in brief

suckling moments of warmth

leading to a climax that

is explosive but too

quickly gone to ever

know what reality is.

I am shattered, broken

and this painful human

condition that is prized

so highly has become

the nightmare of dreams.

and I battle to justify

existence, and I battle

to breathe, and I battle to

believe in even myself

for myself could not

hold the lover, and

even more could not hold

the humanity of

acknowledgement and

yet I called it love

and believed it special.

My ability to think was

pathetically caught up

with the stereotype.

I am not in love, for love is just a word.

Intersection

Did I choose you?

Did you happen?

Does it matter?

Turn right, go left.

Straight ahead is better

but the potholes

are constant

and the scarring,

bloody brutal.

Going back is

now impossible.

Maybe just a little?

Or maybe just a lot?

What do I choose now?

Or, do I let it happen?

Why is the road so hard?

Can someone help me?

Is there a map?

A diagram to direct me.

I need a hand.

I can't do this alone.

Moonlight Deception

Sharply defined you tease my mind.

Distraught with fear I shed a tear.

Inside my heart your words do dart.

I know your name but are you still the same?

Does the word trust taste like rust?

Does the moonlight lie and let the sunlight die?

Are you the link so I can think?

When the madness drifts, will there be rifts?

I am so afraid that myself I cannot upbraid.

This fear is so great it will not abate.

Is it you and the things you do?

Or is it me who has lost the key?

Indifference

I see it all.

Those man-made memories

where joyful explosions of

emotion brings tears,

and laughter.

A reptilian warmth.

I call it orgasm.

It may be real but

it is a fraction only

of the moment that

pleasured time pretends

to us, is more.

I am the frosted ice

of man-made memories

where painful explosions

of emotions bring tears.

Sorrow,

the silken slippery price.

It is an orgasm.
It is a whole lifetime
spotted by blood that
is the moment
pleasure deceives us as
meaningful.
I think I would rather
indifference.
I am weak though
and I will
succumb to hope and
those disruptions will
fragment me till
I am gone.

Adulthood

I grew up today.

I saw truth.

Your eyes are not so nice

and I had to protect

myself.

Truth is truth

but in your being

truth is a lie.

I could have

gone on forever but

I am not yet weak enough

to surrender to the

Cynical Cyclone and let it

destroy all chances that

hope is worth fighting for

and necessary to

my survival.

I win, you lose but

I am now a grown up,

and my heart may

bleed for you but,

I see it now.

I see what is.

Change of Life

I am afraid.

I tremble and cry

silent tears.

I have not the

courage to admit

to those around me that

I am unhappy and so

very sad.

I am powerless to

make changes.

I want to, and

perhaps in knowing that

and in noticing

others too feel this way

I can be less self-indulgent

and leave selfishness behind.

It is selfish to live inside

myself and

deceptive to

think that it

protects me to be

silent.

Missing the Boat

I am an amoeba.
I divide the centuries and flow
in bits and pieces and I multiply
until not even I know
where I go

The human heart,
the physical shape.
The strange complicated
human brain
takes over justifying,
rationalising
till I lose the will
to just explain.

Perplexed, in total confusion
I meander down so many roads
that push and probe at me,

and take me aside.
Good paths, pot-holed paths,
and indifferent ones
causing so much surprise
I am still alive.

Thus, I dissolve
into the scattered parts of
divisions, greedily growing,
exploding into nations.
Wondering always
What is the outcome?
Will there be fruition
from these creations?

Next

The end of the old, and the beginning of the unknown.

Seasons in Turmoil

What happened to Spring?

When did the Summer go?

What was I doing,

to miss the arrival?

How didn't I know?

Autumn,

the best of all.

Autumn,

varied, full of sweet reflections,

and bitter moments and yet

Autumn,

the best of all, magic because

aging, when the process is styled,

has dignity, and the slide from

gold to brown is

a caressing, warming chill

heralding acceptance and

becoming a mentor to all

the things to come, and

the mentor becomes a

friend to all the things left behind.

Every day reaches out

to the brightest stars and their soft,

shining, sprinkled delicate dust adds

a hopeful flavour to the menu the

Universe is still serving.

I am not impatient for the Winter.

I wait, knowing I will find

the comfort of blankets.

Why not?

I bought them a long time ago.

Belonging

Sensations tearing at the internal being.

Connections slow and strong.

Piercing sounds pushed aside.

Deep entrenchment that

calls me back

against my will

to a time and place.

Disparity of skin and speech.

Forceful reality thrown into existence.

Shadows propositioning.

Hidden intricate attachment

that I escaped and

that now ensnares me

to the time and place.

I carry the inhabited weight of

the centuries on my shoulders.

A privilege enveloping and

making me forever

Who

and

What

I am – my birthright.

And at the End

What is there?

A cessation

of the turbulent thinking,

of the mind travelling,

of the constant thoughts

taking me to places

where I never really wanted

to go, not then

and certainly not now.

Is there a nirvana,

of constant achievement

of confused cycles

of random rationality

giving life to individuality

I never really wanted?

Most assuredly not back then

when the energy was higher,

and certainly not now.

Were there choices?
Was there a sanity
of planned purpose?
Did I fail to understand?
Did I choose ambiguous words?
Did I confuse meanings somehow?
Is that why, even now,
there are still steps,
endless, endless steps to climb?

I am more accepting of love and
thankfully I am closer to above.
I had to understand though
to be a little further from below.

People and Wine

Characters we meet

People are like a fine wine

*The barrel chosen,
picked with care, and
perceptive knowledge
lovingly houses and
caresses the aging of
no longer
flowing contents.*

*The rich, unprocessed,
in-depth blend
becomes
the individual housing
the unique flavoured
palette
of personality.*

*Blood-based liquid
drawn from nature's
precious gift and
human sweat combines
with time
to house
treasured and distinctive taste.*

Meet some of my companions

The Adventurer

*Andiamo says the voice inside
for the new is waiting to be tried.
Andiamo means to move and go,
extend our palate with a balanced flow.
A hint of danger, rustic paths to explore.
Lethally addictive bouquet so we want more.*

The Pacifist

Dolce, sweet, a throat balm.
Silent, sliding delicately spreading calm.
Delicious, slowly warming fire
partnering the crisp and tart without the ire
Purity of colour flowing slow.
Refined, pacifying, and worth the know.

The Sensualist

Amore, the ultimate aim,
is sinfully selfish in the goal for fame.
Full-bodied, fleshy perfumes fall,
floating, savouring, lost in the call.
Sensuality oozes, the throat swallows.
Amore in the lingering completion that follows.

The Pleasure Seeker

Man, and wine join and become one.
Desire rules so let the experience be done.
Feel, smell and taste is prime,
and the actions a mouth-filling crime.
Velvet feel, intoxicating aroma
and sinful need leads to a heavenly coma.

The Thinker

Indulgent thoughts will prepare
as the rustic and robust have nostrils flare.
Complexity encourages and moves
as we filter earth and fruit into oaky grooves.
The mind is ready to stop.
Bring on bottle and a glass; time to prop.

And my favourite,

The Conversationalist

Conversing is an exquisite share
for those with aged knowledge to bare.
Discussions will flow as the bottle sits
elegant and ripe with fragrances it emits.
No educational surprises here.
Expecting the best brings satisfaction not fear.

CHERRY BLOSSOMS

Haiku memories

white mountain calls

resolutions in misted ice on lava

fierce movement

beauty in silent idle hands

rippling earth

busy lives encased in concreted skyline glory

honour flutters softly on the harsh past

peaceful warrior heart

smiling warmth abides

hot embers reach limits

cleansing fire rebuilds

differences fade

West and East

misted skins dazzle

fast lane hunger runs

timeless history ambles

true essence prevails

cherry pink blossom

blood on white petals

joyous harmony

Till we meet again, don't be afraid of your emotions, understand them

Barb

Emotions in Evolution

The Poetic Journey Continues

Barbara Strickland

Foreword to Emotions in Evolution (132)

LANDSCAPES (137)

Distanced (139)

No-one gave notice (141)

The F Word (143)

Swimming in deep water (145)

Knock Knock (147)

Senses and Artistry (149)

Natural Inspiration (152)

Dream Worlds (154)

Hush (156)

On backward glances (157)

On loving our children (159)

Reassuring words (160)

Psychic communication (162)

Don't forget to analyse (164)

I am a shadow (166)

Love, it takes all kinds (168)

Losing Love (171)

The Heart and the Alphabet (172)

Outside my window (176)

The Revolution (179)

Resonating changes (181)

Home Sweet Home (183)

A love letter to the girl that was (185)

Gravity gone (186)

All I ever wanted (188)

Making the bed (190)

    TALES OF THE UNEXPECTED (192)

HAIKU AND TRAVEL (193)

    THE COLOUR CONNECTION (204)

THE PRIMARY – The parents (205)

Blue (205)

Red (207)

Yellow (208)

THE SECONDARY – The offspring (209)

Green (209)

Orange (210)

Purple (212)

THE MIX – The resulting generations (214)

Green to Orange (214)

Purple to Black (216)

The Human Hand (218)

THE HAIKU IN COLOUR (220)

THE CINQUAIN IN COLOUR (228)

    THE PLANT CONNECTION (236)

The Carnation (237)

The Daffodil (238)

The Sunflower (239)

The Wisteria (241)

The Ash (242)

PLANTS AND THE HAIKU (244)

PLANTS AND THE CINQUAIN (250)

Foreword to Emotions in Evolution

I have surprised myself by wanting to do another poetry book. Then again, maybe I am not so surprised. The freedom poetry allows is addictive, liberating and an adrenalin donation I was not expecting. For me poetry is a welcome donor to my ever growing, need for energy.

The world is ravenous for our energy. Being busy is the normal these days, but tired people lose creativity. Evolution can only come and thrive from fresh and creative approaches in all aspects of our lives. We need to nurture whatever feeds our energy. For me the addition of poetry has been quite a revelation. When I finish a piece, I feel energised, like a weight has lifted I didn't know I carried.

I have looked at the world as a series of landscapes as you will see. The topics within this are random. The commonality is always the evolution of emotions. Emotions are our connection to each other, and I like that connection. In my first poetry book my emotions erupted, in this they are on the road to evolving.

Attempting to put my small stamp on an art form that humbles me is challenging and satisfying. Putting words together in a disciplined form clarifies perspective, overhauls your mind-set. Mine certainly needed that to happen. I can't help wondering if others out there feel the same. Selfishly I find that an exciting and invigorating idea.

If you have read Emotions in Eruption you will know I have a love for the Haiku. I was and still am a novice but the determination to master it grows daily. I love the stunning simplicity of the form and it has led me to embrace the Cinquain. This too thrives on simplicity but allows a little more room for expression. Both forms clamour for the right choice of words. I confess I am addicted to the structure of both these forms. The following is a little bit of information you might find interesting. My research is still in the early stages and in any case, I was more interested in the essence of these two forms.

The Haiku, Japanese in origin, is based on a pattern of syllables. Traditionally it is broken into three lines of five syllables, seven syllables, and five syllables on the last line, however stress is different for the Japanese language. It makes sense that we needed to re-think things. These days the form is not so strict. Often a haiku can be one or two lines in length. The important thing is to be concrete and concise. A haiku will capture a single moment in just a few words and do it with rich imagery. The goal with a haiku is the creation of an image in the mind of the reader, one celebrating beauty and nature with sensitivity.

The challenge to achieve this, whilst difficult, is also something that plucks the best from the poet's imagination. It draws the aspiring poet into a world where expressing emotions in a condensed fashion becomes an all-consuming fever. The haiku makes any topic a source of inspiration and cuts through human experience and cultural boundaries. I love bonsai for the same reason. You can express so much through the smaller, more delicate form, you can encapsulate emotion. I have tried to walk both the traditional path, and one in which I have experimented. Please, bear in mind I am a novice and comments are most welcome.

The cinquain, on the other hand, is an example of shape poetry, and one demanding a more exact number of words for each line of the five lines required. This rigidity creates a unique, symmetrical shape with interesting and descriptive words. However, with the passing of time variable have arisen and these often appear contradictory. I decided I would take the essence and adopt the style often used in schools to get student creative juices flowing. The first word is a noun and forms the title. The second line consists of two adjectives and the third consists of three 'ing' participles. The fourth line is a phrase and then the last line another noun. This must be a synonym for the title word. The restrictions are like a puzzle. Instead of pieces we position words in a manner that allows them to be autonomous narrators.

Along with these two poetry forms came a fascination for colour in nature. The different shades and depths spoke of stories and I wondered if I could use colour as a muse, and if colour itself was enough. Linking it to life began to make sense. Colours are everywhere in nature. Do individual colours have a meaning? I found that they have, they have a surprisingly extensive vocabulary of their own, as do plants. They have a vocabulary and an incredible history. Plants have long been used medicinally and often nefariously in in magic.

And then I had another thought, what about flowers? They are conspicuously present on birthdays, funerals, graduation and weddings, thus forming an integral part of our lives. Most people know a red rose stands for romantic love and that one does not send yellow roses to anyone in mourning. Most people don't consider flower meanings but when I checked I found some amazing results. Like plants, they have their own aligned meanings, creating a language all their own.

Bombarded with possibilities, I found myself caught in a sudden thunderstorm without an umbrella. Drops of rain beat down hitting my skin, each drop screaming with an idea of its very own, including a link to my novels. Travel is a big part of my books and I wondered whether I could narrow down the individuality of different countries into the smoothness of seventeen syllables. It turned out to be fun trying.

Have I done a good job manipulating words and emotions? You decide, and feel free to let me know what you think. I would be most delighted to make changes, improvements and take new ideas on board. Already I have new ideas for new forms of poetry to explore, so stop me while you can.

Welcome to Emotions in Evolution

Barbara Strickland 2018

Landscapes
(The World in Verse)

The world in which we live dictates our behaviour, influences the way we think. The world however is complex and made up of divisions, both subtle and obvious, conflicting and confusing and blurring the lines where limits might exist. Those divisions come with impressive resumes, demanding we pay attention, for they too are story tellers and they hold our past and lead us to our future.

We have the physical world, the one that exists around us, man-made, and different to the natural one showcasing landforms, oceans, flora and fauna. And then, there is the world of dreams, our hopes and desires, soul felt and creating an emotional rollercoaster. Lastly there is the controversial supernatural where believers of magic connect. This one we call the psychic realm and its mystical fingers keep us fascinated.

We live and love within these boundaries; they shape us and define us. For me personally they create inspiration to form the collection of words you find on these pages. My thoughts are random and roam each landscape with eyes that feed a brain in evolution.

Distanced

I lay dying.

No-one

to see.

I lay despairing.

No-one

to listen.

I lay disassociated.

No-one

to care.

When did the lane disintegrate?

When did the path diverge?

When did the road dissipate?

When did the highway dissolve?

When did the freeway disappear?

Talking is not the enemy.

It is the way of the traveller.

No one gave notice

Breathing has become impossible.
The automatic flow now my dead
dearest friend.
Hidden and obstructed
fuelling fires flame
growing, grieving, grasping
holding hard hopelessly
to life lost, unwanted.

Thinking has become anguished.
The unstoppable flow now my live
worst enemy.
Obvious, in full view
the fleeting feelings freeze
groaning grievously grim
heaving hurling horror

for life gone, unrealised.

Where was the warning bell?

Did the landlord forget to give notice?

The F Word

Fear, fright, frigid

fickle, failure, frozen

freedom, flying, feeling

fractious, frenzied, flippant

fashionable, fantastic, fabulous

fleeing, fighting, and falling.

Fragrantly fresh friendships and

freakishly fierce foes.

Words are wispy wisdom.

Words are withered wickedness.

Words are simple silent speakers.

Words are slithering in superficial sounds.

They just flow.

They just exist.

They don't always rhyme

but they can be

manipulating, manoeuvring, mangling

masked mutilators.

They can be

magical, magnificent, meanings

moving mountains.

Why the fuck then, do we choose

a vicious verbal twist so that

semantics become syntax-shaped

weapons creating the

fucking fearful clothed figures

of language failure?

Humane humility, or

'h' words are

so much

nicer.

Swimming in deep water

I float;

my face uplifted.

I drown;

the water shifted.

The pull was strong

and called my name.

I recognised a siren song

from whence it came

but I was not

confident.

I failed to fight.

I am not yet

solvent

and am blinded by light.

I am a weak human creation.

I truly do my best

to ignore the clawing sensation

as I fail each test.

To survive you must make the dive.

That's right, isn't it?

The day to thrive will arrive.

That's true, isn't it?

Knock, knock

I hear the words inside my head.

My sleep broken,

I resist

the incessant pull

until

the tugging pains me,

the force annoys me.

Knock, knock.

Nobody home

but

I hate lies,

I hate self-deceit,

I hate the constant buzz,

and

I give in.

I give up.

I write it down.

I write them down.

Knock, knock.

Words are calling.

Senses and Artistry

A heady seductive combination

of words and senses.

An intoxicating mixture

thoughtfully chosen so

the intricate infused joining is

a harmonious fixture.

Smell reaches out, reaches in

and fills our hearts

with a fragrant pull to please

or to assail like painful sin.

The eager eyes await their turn

to feature in the artistry of

unfolding senses with dazzling colours

to have us learn.

Unconfined the sense of feel,
Of touch, distinguishes between
satin and silk and mineral earth
recognising what is real.

The ears, two tiny shells,
hide from shrieking voices or
bask joyously in music and
clearly defined distant bells.

The tongue, a human elemental,
reaches out to sweet and sour
tantalising and maximising chilli heat
with the blend of spicy oriental.

Sensory artistry whispers
to the waiting words
and asks for the wisdom

to create unique places

and fairy tale moments within

our very own earthly kingdom.

Natural Inspiration

Around me,

surrounds me.

For there is magic

filling my pores,

taking over my senses

on the green hued floors

of sprouting leaves and roots,

inside stick-like branches

and in natural lawns

of fresh smelling and smiling fields.

I seek their calm.

I am avarice for the peace

of different shades that

blend beckoningly, battling

the never ceasing contrasting

seams of bounty the humans only lease.

I seek possession.

I am anxious for title deeds,

for proving ownership

and having rights, and

to reach ruin without replenishing.

Quiet! I hear voices, a question!

Did someone call Earth a rental?

Dream Worlds

There are so many.

Where do we start?

If we choose wrong,

we'll break a heart.

There's the one we want,

the one we crave,

but don't go there

or are you brave?

I'm not. It frightens me.

It lures with promises

and disguises the pitfalls

with romantic premises.

There's the one we call a fantasy.

It's the one where we dare

to dream of the things

we're afraid to share.

Only the hopeful will admit

their thoughts are continuous

and fixated on it.

There's the world where we live.

It's real, it's every day.

It's where I stay.

Those other worlds are not for me.

My mind is locked away without a key.

Hush

Silence, the constant glow of

media light of unending power

in the recesses that never fill,

in the tunnels that lead nowhere, everywhere.

Where did the symphonic sounds of

melodic, maniacal madness go?

Is there a simultaneous event in action?

Is there a juxtaposition

hammering in my head?

There exists a silence of absence.

It is most kind, most respectful.

There is a silence of unheard words.

It is most cruel and most merciless.

On backward glances

Dangerous aging memories

of

an amazing time that bleakly flew,

call you.

Wishing is an unsafe toy

and

regret – a stupid, useless ploy.

Content in a world that moved along

you foolishly turned,

caught up in reckless recollections.

In emotional tethers tangling tenaciously

you glanced in that gilded gold glass

where

you no longer belonged

and

saw torn and tattered lace

and a wrinkled saddened

colour-lacking face.

Time is cruel, brutalising

and

the feathered softness

of

the quilted past

shows bleak, bottomless baffled

eyes

unfocused, downcast

and

the consequence

of

all those lies.

On loving our children

A natural task

but the little horrors wear a mask.

Angelic when they sleep –

by day they write on walls

and make you weep.

They cuddle close and hold on tight

then deny it when they bite.

They fail to see crumbs bring ants galore

and deny spilled drinks bring you more.

Cruel and sweet, kiss or beat,

their challenge a feat and hard to meet

and yet, for them our hearts do beat.

Reassuring sounds

I heard the clock tick.

How strange when

silence of technology

rules.

I heard my heartbeat.

And, I pondered for

loneliness of being

reigns.

I heard the dripping of blood.

And, I shut my eyes

against the fear power

commands.

I heard the forced expulsion of breath

and I chose to whimper

ceding all my hard won

control.

I heard the change to nothing.

And I answered with nothing for

stillness had come home to

reside.

My body belongs to the puppeteer.

My mind knows only to follow.

Un-coordinated, unable to resist

the final fear I swallow.

Thank you for turning off the machine.

Psychic communication

The connections take me prisoner.

I can't avoid the sun, the moon

and the sky above, and

the air I breathe.

The land holds me,

grounds me and gives me life.

I am a part of it,

a part of the greater,

a part of the more

I don't understand.

They, it, all that it is

holds me

with its power.

For the world is magical

and if I honour its apparitions

then power will yield

to me and I will

commune with the universe

and not just the world

around me.

Don't forget to analyse

Soundless whispers are welcome.

Alone in our mind

the truth gets caught

forcing out

the troubled thought,

twisting it, turning it

into things best left unsaid

leaving our soul unfed.

Don't look so hard!

Don't turn around!

Certainly, most of all

don't make a sound.

Ignore what you can.

Accept what is possible

for you,

a mortal man.

For we are told

that to question

interprets too often

as far too bold.

What then?

Oblivion?

It is good to comprehend.

Wise to hesitate before pressing send.

Despite what appears an obvious link

there is a necessity

telling us to stop and think.

Analysing improves capacity

our brains expand and forgo the Shrink.

I am a shadow

Faded, worn and lost

because the process makers

ignore the aging cost.

I am a wraith

almost transparent now.

My colours blur and dilute

and my spirit despairs

at the naivety of the so called astute.

I am a whisper of wind

to voices, lingeringly loud

demanding the attention,

the rights of the belligerent proud.

And suddenly it matters not

that they forgot.

For I have dissipated,

have been obliterated

and now to my surprise

finally

I am liberated.

Love, it takes all kinds

The Greeks had seven words for love, and I thought I might explore this in prose. My leading lady Alexia in Unexpected Passion is Greek, and I think she is exerting a greater influence than I first suspected. I hope so as she is quite the character.

The bane of our existence.

The reason for our evolution.

The reason for human persistence.

The emotion that lacks solution.

The Ancient Greeks gave us insight.

Separated views of love have might.

Eros was erotic and sexual.

Agape selfless and sacrificial.

Ludus played, flirted, seduced.

Philia to friendship, platonic was reduced.

Pragma we all hope to obtain

for Pragma is shared love and

the one we all hope to retain.

Why not, when it means

long-standing, a couple's refrain.

And now we move to self-love

or Philautia by name.

A puzzle, often a nuisance from above

when narcissism is the game.

But then self-love can be enabling

giving us a noble redemption

when we lose the ego labelling

with caring as our intention.

And when Storge deems to reveal

we find the best is last

for familial has nothing to conceal

as parent and child, love holds fast.

What now, we ask?

Do divisions ease the task?

But love remains the eternal mystery

controlling lives all through our history.

Losing Love

Drifting slow and hitting fast

from the awful spell you cast

I move away and hope to keep

the sorrow from burrowing

into my soul so deep.

You didn't listen as I spoke,

refused what I chose to evoke.

I sat quietly and replied

and hid the telling sounds I sighed.

How many times now has agony fed

upon the failure of what I said?

The Heart and the Alphabet

Wings whispering,

earnest exchanging,

harsh hammering,

angry advancing,

deadly dancing,

useless urging

outside my skin,

and inside my head.

My beating heart,

is confused but keeps up.

Clouds circling,

softly singing,

ornate offering,

gently gifting,

peaceful pondering,

quiet questioning,

inside my skin,

and outside my head.

My beating heart needs

to settle down.

Talons tingling,

madly menacing,

vicious venting,

ragged reasoning,

keenly kicking,

laborious listening,

outside my skin,

and inside my head.

My beating heart is confused again

and speeds up.

Feathers fluttering,

innocent idling,

bashful believing,

noiseless nodding,

youthful yielding,

judicious juggling,

inside my skin,

and outside my head.

My beating heart splutters,

slowing down.

The scales are weighted,

balanced, and fair.

The heart is not sold,

won't credit images as fated,

won't listen, doesn't dare,

wants it to end, to fold.

Inside, outside the skin.

Inside, outside the head.

The puzzle pieces are thin.

Zing. The heart stops.

Zap. The heart is dead.

Outside my window

Little bird, little bird,

go find somewhere else to play.

I hate your cheeping voice.

Find somewhere far away

because quiet is my choice.

I want to dream, to sleep,

not listen to the high-pitched call.

Yet I hear it, I hear it creep,

wanting, daring to enthral.

It has awakened my heart

with its trill and flapping wings.

It has pierced the deepest part.

It has that power when it sings.

Does the winged one call

because I am feeling sad?

Does it deliberately enthral

because it wants me glad?

No light fills my heart

despite the power of those wings.

Sharp ear piercing on its part

despite the pretty way it sings.

It knows I need to take the leap

and refuses to let me ignore his call.

It knows my unhappiness is deep

and knows I need it to enthral.

Little bird, little bird,

don't leave, don't go away.

I was very wrong.

I can't start my day

without your sweet, sweet song.

The Revolution

Listen. Listen to the rain.

Listen as it falls.

Pay attention to the wind.

Listen as it calls.

Listen. Listen to each other.

Break down those walls.

Pay close attention to the truth.

before it palls.

Evolution or a revolution?

Listen. Listen to the land.

Listen as it rumbles.

Pay attention to the sea.

Listen as it tumbles.

Listen. Listen to the earth.

Watch as the human fumbles.

Pay close attention to our earth

before it crumbles.

Reconstruction or deconstruction?

If we listen to the revolution

we may just reach our evolution.

If we don't think about deconstruction

we may never get to reconstruction.

Resonating Changes

Polar bears are drowning.

I heard that somewhere.

Suddenly I was frowning

And awake enough to care.

What action will it take

for it to truly resonate?

What disruption must we make

for us to truly question fate?

For everything else we do,

we stop to make a plan or two.

Seems strange to hesitate.

Seems odd to refuse the date

when all the earth begs to ask

is a portion of our love

choosing, a small but valid task,

to keep the sky above,

CLEAN.

When all the earth begs to ask,

is a portion of our busy day

choosing, a small but valid task

to preserve our oceans where we play,

CLEAN.

It begins in our home.

It starts with us, alone.

It spreads in rapid haste.

Preventing thoughtless waste.

Find your polar bear.

Find your way to care.

Home sweet home

Buildings made of steel,

stone, plaster, cement, low-rise

or high-rise. Wait a minute,

aren't those blue jeans?

Bricks, mortar, timber

and re-enforced glass,

all materials, creating,

establishing, an abode

from which to look at

the world, and consider

the world and maybe,

one to keep us safe.

Hay, mud, animal skins,

leaves, tree trunks, sand,

caves, holes underground, and

tunnels, boats large and small.

Well, the places exist.

What makes an abode,

a habitat – a home?

Well, it appears we forgot the

people. Was that deliberate?

Heaven becomes hell

And the oasis drifts back to desert.

A love letter to the girl that was

It starts as a rose bud.

Tiny tender petals

of youth, of not knowing,

until the bud explodes.

And the sweet, untouched flesh

bleeds with longing as it settles.

There were thorns that lingered,

thorns that pricked,

the unsuspecting digits.

Thorns, not only daring to grasp,

but arrogantly and greedily, fingered.

We took without asking,

assuming our fingerprints had rights

to the leaves of forever young, and

we tainted, misappropriated

while sunshine basking.

Gravity gone

Sometimes I feel the planet

Spinning, turning without me.

Months go by and I

don't understand where the

days, nights have gone.

I don't know where I am

not to feel the pull of gravity,

not to feel my soul cemented to

my body's casing.

Am I in space?

Have I gone, to another world,

another dimension?

No, I am here.

I am alone.

This is what brittles the bone,

despite the hand-held phone

supposedly holding all the voices

with visiting choices.

What a sad refrain

when friends forget

to say your name.

What a cruel, god damned shame.

All I ever wanted

It should have been easy.

It should have flowed.

I'll bet that's what they all said

until the rules were read.

We weren't told it had been decided.

They couldn't chance the questions.

They couldn't allow the impression

that could lead to apprehension.

They prohibited the word, anarchy.

Instead they invented the term, solitary.

That's where I currently reside

and where most days I choose to hide.

All I ever wanted was a peaceful life

but instead I found a well-sharpened knife.

Maybe that's how it's meant to be

and all I ever wanted is right here in front of me.

A choice would have been nice.

Making the bed

Wake up. Time for life.

Stay asleep. It's far less strife.

I have things I have to do.

Really? Are you sure that's true?

I move. I leave the warmth.

I move again. I leave safety.

I move once more. I hesitate and shake.

Does what I do matter?

I'm already in pieces.

What more can I shatter?

Everything I own has creases.

I turn and make the bed.

I'm alive. Today I thrive.

It's better than the alternate dead.

191

Quiet, I tell my mind.

Please try to be a little kind.

Please just this once, stop the constant natter.

I sigh as the freshly made bed diminishes the pitter patter.

Tales of the Unexpected

A Haiku reflection on the great fortune I have experienced travelling to wonderful places. My characters in The Unexpected Series (a contemporary, and a little erotic, romance series) will be fortunate enough to do the same.

Haiku and Travel

Tuscan beauty

enfolds our vision and captures hearts

medieval charm

a fragrant sweep of wine implodes

Venetian glass

glistening gondola glide

bridges sigh

eons of enchanted southern warmth

Mediterranean Sea

Roman Hills cry and whisper timeless tears

of history

dark Gothic remains

Renaissance and Byzantine flavours

travellers return to the golden isle

Sicilian sun

amphitheatre

Olympian laurel green

challenge accepted

ancient hierarchy of ruins

columns standing straight and bold

Turkish taste delight

colourful spice markets smell sweet

Byzantine tiles

arrogant storytelling in mosaic patterns

Rheine Castles

magical dark green woods

rippling river flow

clean deep inhale

snow kissed Swiss alpine glory

Vienna woods

atmospheric music in listening leaves

Spanish fiesta

furious flashing Flamenco feet

Portuguese red wine splendour

the Pyrenees call to taste

bonjour sweet pastry

embracing city lovers Parisian style

Nordic gods' splendour

cascade of pure ice

fresh cleansed breath

tulip blanket bold

classic wooden shoes ride proud bicycle paths

London calling card

Big Ben and Convent Garden with fish and chips

Stonehenge majesty

thousands of years held ransom by green fields

Scottish lairds rule

purple rolling hills

Loch Ness myths

Jerusalem hails unique

city of white perched placid and pure

dates in the desert

parched mouths and dry lips breathe in the oasis

salt encrusted sea

memories float inside skins of the avaricious

exotic energy

Casablanca dream

cold marbled magic

pyramid dunes

buried parts and golden desert merge into an oasis

cherry pink scented

blush and bloom

Japanese treasure

Singapore sights

night zoo and orchid garden

monsoon deluge

Harbour Bridge

Opera House and Blue Mountains sing a Sydney song

Great Barrier Reef

coral views in glass-bottomed boats

turtles

coast of soft silken sand

surfers ride the weaving waves

Australian gold

rainy days

tram travel and city grid

Melbourne glamour

The Colour Connection

Red, yellow, and blue are known as primary colours. Together they create secondary colours. Combining results within those combinations create tertiary colours. It is a complex process that brings a diversity to brighten our lives.

I have always had a soft spot for the Romantic Poets and their love for Nature. Already fascinated by colours and the way they bring life to our world, I wondered if I could put words to the blending and combining, the perfecting of each hue and the embedding of meaning to warm and comfort us.

I wanted to give a voice to the colour connection through the haiku (traditional and more modern), the cinquain and some free verse.

The Primary – The Parents

Blue

Half the world we see

is sky, is ocean.

You hold the key,

the magic potion

of flow, of open spaces

and the freshness of cool

gliding on our faces.

Your colour is an endless pool

where man can dive

and revive.

Blue shades twist and creep

ruling hard with water might.

Liquid leaves the fathoms deep

and sea and sky begin their fight,

ensuring that our planet grows

and the cycle of life evolves,

continuing its highs and lows

as each drop of rain dissolves.

Encouragement for man to strive

and to survive.

Red

Some would argue the powers of hell

hold the reins, ring the bell.

Red is the unquenchable fire

and some would argue, heaven's sire.

Red is gluttonous, holding every need

for only it allows, the possibility to feed.

The hues, the variegated soils,

the sly fox lava underground that boils,

the bitter cutting edges of unshaped rocks,

the vicious cold tunnels where treasure mocks,

reminds us that fragile humans are merely limbs,

helpless against wicked self-indulgent whims.

Yellow

The warmth of the universe in measured spread

melts through the night until the dark is shed.

Uplifting the spirits and creativity,

teasing away all responsibility.

Yellow is the morning sun.

Yellow comes when the damp is done,

cleansing, clearing, and even purifying

for the golden light is sweetly satisfying.

Honeybees share the splendour,

kissing soft slick petals as they meander

seeking perfect pollen sustenance

in recycled reproduction romance.

And the gentle burn of the magic ray

coming from places so far away

gives life to mountain tops, stream fed rivers,

Green fields, blue skies, and even human divas.

The Secondary – The Offspring

Green

Green, green, nature's might.

Lemon-skinned lime with an olive bite.

Apple streaks, emerald lights

of harmony and nurturing sights,

and legacies of honoured heights.

Nature cleanses so humans survive

the poison to our breathing

that growls, harshly seething

as green velvet keeps us alive.

In return we lack appreciation

and the beauty we abound in

shows a depreciation,

an almost unearthly sin.

Orange

Superb sunset and

stunning sunrise.

Orange is flamboyant,

a hostess for nature's

more excitable moments.

Desert stone takes on a fiery

festive assertion

standing proud in

Australian territory.

Fire glow and heat provider

fuelling volcanic tempers

changing adventurous rumblings

into exhibitionist explosions.

You feed red; you ignore green

but peach softens your reaction

while proud amber seeks

jewelled superficial satisfaction

and is blind to the power of blue.

Communication is on your terms,

opportunist confidence only too true.

Purple

Purple, you tell a story

with richness and splendour.

From mystic amethyst gracing

the human with glory

to the majesty of deep magenta

and the violet stained-glass placing.

Purple, you inspire the imagination.

Yet with an arrogant stance

your hues turn into deluded grandeur

fraught with pompous, cynical corruption

until deep spirituality asks for a dance

and you forgive the immature.

In fields of flowers, lilac dwells

with heather hills in competition.

The lavender evening sky stakes a claim

then sunset's royal shade preens and swells.

Dignified, it allows evening succession

from the mauve palette to dark plum fame.

The Mix – The Resulting Generation

Green to Orange

I cover the earth in:

brilliant emerald,

lengthening grassy green,

deeply darkened jade.

And, all of them fade

to a frantic fruity lime

or an olive grove glow

until the searching sea recycled,

acquiescing into aqua flow.

I acknowledge my centre:

amber glides in beaded glory,

a peach perfect gleam has a say.

So many colours for us to see

all mixing with volcanic glee.

Golden gilded gifts from a

centred orange furnace has

yellow flecks show their face

and in the pale heat of a fired ember

night smiles as sunrise takes its place.

Purple to Black

I look around enthralled.

Nature has provided life.

Lilac flowers breathe their scent

a pale modest muted bent.

Vibrancy arrives to ripen plums.

An evolved admired amethyst stone

processes red and blue into proven purple

in the stunning sweetness of sunsets shown.

Lovingly the pretty palette spreads,

the blended shades a symphony

where earth's dirt is dusted brown

and sable sands don't quite frown.

Then with care, ivory leaches white

allowing grey to cloud the atmosphere

to a bloated blasphemous black

before the sudden summer storms appear.

And it begins again.

The Human hand

We take a tube

and squeeze

using long thin greedy fingers.

A fisted curiosity lingers.

Rainbow colours grow by our hand

yet if we chance to step away

and just peruse the land

we see that nature has every day

shown us a better blend

to seize.

We watch

and reflect.

Where the brush had our digits curl

now slowly we choose to unfurl.

We copy what is already there,

opening our eyes wide, to see.

We comprehend our gathered fare

as nature bestows the treasured key

and kindly allows us

the grand, the very full effect.

The Haiku in Colour

(blending nature with the personalities of colour)

Colour me Blue

sky talk

tender blue white patches

grey grizzles

waves ripple

muddy grey to ocean blue

salt crystals

white softness

bubbles in the blue horizon

Colour me Red

passionate desire

liquid lava flow

heated destruction

warm sunshine on skin

dissipating red rays leave blemishes

the goddess Venus

distant and unforgiving planet of flames

Colour me Green

Green balance

gentle hands rejuvenate

tranquillity

palest new leaf

baby footprints expand

tangled jade scenes

green expanses

peace

lady-in-waiting

Colour me Yellow

sunshine cheerful

citrus floral stimulant

daylight vibrancy

lemon taste tickles

simulated gold on a waiting tongue

fourth finger

left hand

yellow banded vows

Colour me Purple

soft purple haze

rich flowering lavender

mystic carpet

lilac summer night

bright muted-rainbow-touched sunsets

outrageous mauve

free spirited crimson mutation

Colour me Pink

Unconditional pink

positive female energy

flirtations

passionate lovers in fuchsia

Colour me Orange

orange socialiser

dawn breaker night seducer

frantic fire

orange flames rise proud

volcano

The Cinquain in Colour

(colour meanings in action)

Red

Energetic, passionate

Stimulating, motivating, dominating

Waits with dark intensity

Power

Burgundy

Rich, sophisticated

Reigning, controlling, determining

Ambition with dignity

Regal

Crimson

Bright, beautiful

Enticing, teasing, tantalising

Emitting sexual intensity

Blood

Maroon

Strong, positive

Pondering, reflecting, wondering

Controlled thinking

Thoughtful

Blue

Conservative, predictable

Enhancing, calming, healing

Whispered wings of wisdom

Peace

Turquoise

Balance, Stability

Communicating, clarifying, recharging

Enhancer of empathy

Idealism

Navy

Conservative, compassionate

Repressing, worrying, regulating

Non-demonstrative and non-emotional entity

Corporate

Aqua

Thoughtful, honest

Refreshing, cooling, enveloping

Universally admired

Freedom

Yellow

Impatient, vibrant

Stimulating, creating, investigating

Bringing clarity to the mind

Sunshine

Orange

Sociable, playful

Rejuvenating, self-indulging, overbearing

Stimulating appetite and conversation

Optimism

Citrine

Fickle, superficial

Teasing, deceiving, retreating

Serial hopper of emotions

Unstable

Lemon

Sensitive, wary

Self-relying, cleaning, clearing

Fears the critical

Orderly

Purple

Unusual, individual

Dreaming, dignifying, meditating

Superior and regally royal

Imagination

Lavender

Fragile, sensitive

Aspiring, romancing, idolising

Muted purple power

Vulnerable

Amethyst

Concerned, decisive

Protecting, opening, evolving

A sensitive mystic soul

Humanitarian

Indigo

Intuitive, idealistic

Knowing, maintaining, conforming

Self-mastery supports structure

Contentment

The Plant Connection

Plants have long held special meanings. Each plant is individual and unique and if we listen carefully it will tell us a story of magic and medicine and of times gone by.

The carnation

Your abundance of colour

delights the eye.

Each one a symbol

a story to apply.

Loving, admiring, rejecting.

Disdainful whilst perfecting

capricious purple, and mother love pink

is multi-faceted to make us think.

Give me white and know me pure.

Give me red full of allure.

Golden yellow may disappoint some,

and stripes may give a refusal outcome.

Encompassing plentiful and colour-varied faces,

the carnation speaks of beautiful places.

The Daffodil

So pretty, so complicated,

your meaning is almost variegated.

On your own, misfortune speaks.

Bring a bunch and you have joy,

but unrequited love seeks

new beginnings to employ.

Your delicate petals indicate rebirth.

Your ability to return suggests life eternal.

Standing in a long straight line,

buried in soft sweet earth

your chivalry can't help but shine.

reaching out from within to the external.

The Sunflower

Standing tall and on guard.

Sun lover, rich with yellow gold.

Seeds of courage carried into battle

or pounded powder to spirit hold.

You are versatile.

Your rounded shape a timekeeper,

a classically designed sundial,

bending as the heat hits your open face

to the delight of the harvester on hand

glowing at your offered treats.

Oil for cooking or medicinal

ailment curing, or magic feats,

or as a dye for lustreless cloth

a cooking classic cultivated for

its capability to be

so much more.

The Wisteria

I am wisteria.

I symbolise love and longevity,

bliss and tender immortality

with my gift of sensitivity.

I support, and I give

as I strive to live.

Consciousness to expand the vine

I share in abundance the purple line

of flowering blooms in their glory

allowing all to enjoy my story.

The Ash

Standing tall and strong,

the Ash sings a symbolic song.

The past, present and future blend

telling us of the rules that bend

as roots flow and spread,

when worlds join by a string, a thread.

The underworld comes first,

then middle earth with a burst.

Last to unite and to agree

is the one we too often fail to see,

the strange realm of the spiritual

badly needed to seal the mutual.

An equality in co-existence seals our fate

and helps rid us of unwanted freight.

The Ash stands tall and strong and steers man away from wrong.

Plants and the Haiku
(sharing history and meaning)

inspiring lotus

mental illuminator

cleared minds open

mandrake root

human negativity and bringer of curses

majestic poison

spellbinding charismatic oleander charm

fairies

Four-leaf-clover with fortune and fidelity

purification

grounded human emotions

parsley

rue be thy plant name

governor of sadness and depression

raspberry preserve

protective love and soil fertility offering

Ginseng enhancer

focused clarity of the mind

rainmaker pixie

eternal knowledge

archaic rich fern

liquid slow maple flow

sugar sweet longevity

pennyroyal plant

noble peace protector with majestic stature

salicylic acid and aspirin

bark baskets

willow sprigs

lily modesty

sweetness and purity of heart and soul

haughty heights

sunflower soldiers pay homage to the sun

twelve red roses

fragrant longing for love

chaste white rosebud

woman in mantilla lace splendour

sunshine warm

platonic evocation

yellow rose

mixed coloured buds

rose spawned emotions

taste of maybes

heathered lavender

gothic tales span wild solitary moors

tree roots

blood blackened striped veins

Mother Earth

Shadowed darkness

Elm markers repulse

Tainted woods

temperance

true representation

azalea modesty

Plants and the Cinquain

Knowledge

Ancient, smooth

Writing, wishing, replacing

Grained surface word carrier

Beech

Paradox

Powerful, deceptive

Stimulating, sedating, contradicting

Cat magic and spell maker

Catnip

Leaves

Three, four

Balancing, succeeding, protecting

Luck bringer and fairy viewer

Clover

Divination

Chaotic, random

Lusting, loving, repelling

Fertile five pretty petals

Hibiscus

Prophetic

Clumsy, awkward

Strengthening, healing, protecting

Inferring by astral projection

Mugwort

Catalyst

Magic, sacred

Hunting, exorcising, fertilising

Loved by Druids

Mistletoe

Flute

Flexible, musical

Expanding, budding, symbolising

Music making stalks

Reed

Tree

Versatile, dominant

Conducting, storing, growing

Earth elemental bargain

Spruce

Passion

Symbolic, lucky

Loving, tempting, rewarding

Creating love spells

Strawberry

Potion

Strong, youthful

Loving, energising, boosting

Druid power plant

Vervain

Faith

Shy, peaceful

Retiring, wishing, healing

Hiding behind the larger picture

Violet

Manners

Cultured, spellbinder

Stabilising, purifying, invoking

Safety in an unstable environment

Waterlily

Psychic

Dangerous, poisonous

Protecting, inducing, harming

Caller of spirits

Wormwood

Healer

Cool, protective

Soothing, calming, refreshing

Breaker of hexes

Wintergreen

Herb

Strong, pure

Healing, regenerating, aiding

Sealer of wounds

Bloodroot

Cleanser

Healthy, Healing

Exorcising, protecting, anti-thieving

Curbing poisons and disease spread

Juniper

Treasure

Hidden, Chaste

Enduring, protecting, adapting,

Environmental water storage

Cactus

Useful

Versatile, protective

Hex-breaking, growing, wishing

Fortune and safety

Bamboo

Wisdom

Open-minded, experienced

Curing, protecting, long-living

Basket maker and spiritual protector

Willow

Ceremonial

Generous, provident

Cleansing, prospering, healing

Amulets and medicinal bundles

Cedar

Till next time, be kind to plants and love colours, treasure them because they have magic

Barbara

Emotions in Existence

The Poetic Journey

never ends

Barbara Strickland

Foreword Emotions in Existence (266)

Eruption, Evolution and Existence (271)

PLAYING WITH WORDS (273)

A LOVE SONNET OR TWO, MY WAY (274)

First Love (274)

Love and Sin (276)

Real Love (278)

Love thrice (280)

A sonnet to the Master (282)

I wander and I wonder (284)

A MELODY OF VERSE DEVICES (286)

Poetry (286)

Poets (286)

The Poetic Triangle (287)

Inversion of the Poetic Triangle (287)

More than a Metaphoric Phrase (289)

Self-Destruction: a narrative (291)

An Ode to Words (293)

LET'S GO FREESTYLE (295)

Habits (295)

Depressed Differences (297)

CT Scan 299)

The Forgetful Ones (302)

On the Edge (305)

Accepting the Reality (307)

Anger Management (310)

Running Away (312)

Wrong Turn (315)

Yesterday, Today and Tomorrow (317)

Outsider (319)

Parking the Car (321)

I have a place (325)

The Boomerang Effect (327)

An Italo-Australian (328)

Oops, I messed up again (330)

Oops, I messed up again, again (332)

Humanality (335)

The Box (337)

Technology (339)

The Loner Red Rose (341)

The Circle of Life (343)

The Intellectual Lover's Game (346)

Falling Rain: a reflection of human nature (348)

Sunset comes calling (351)

HAIKU MAGIC (353)

Random Ramblings (354)

Tales of the Unexpected (366)

Lovers and Books and The Unexpected Series (367)

Travel and The Unexpected Series (369)

TANKA TALK (374)

CHERITA CHERISHING (378)

HAIBUN HAPPENS (386)

Foreword Emotions in Existence

The reality of emotions is that they erupt, often when we least expect it. Sometimes they evolve, sometimes they don't. The one thing we can count on is their existence, and so Emotions in Existence came to life. One poetry book was overwhelming yet here I am with a trilogy, well, not exactly a trilogy but close enough.

Humbly I hope that in writing this third book my learning is reflected, and I have learned a great deal, along this poetic journey – about writing, about emotions, about myself and my fears and doubts, and about the joys found in simple things. Learning impacts, changes and improves how things are said, and learning makes the journey so much better than the destination.

In this last book I wanted the freedom to explore ideas about existence, I wanted an opportunity to play with words, shapes and types of poems using different mediums without worrying about themes. You will however find emotions are a recurring thread and be warned, I do wander into the darker side of emotions. We have them and too often we are afraid to express them. For me there is comfort when what I read resonates, explains or clarifies.

But don't worry, I also delve into nature, colours, and let the haiku takes us travelling once more. In fact, I felt like a tourist making new discoveries, writing this. I took small forays into sonnets, into poetic devices, shapes and free verse before moving onto Japanese poetry. As a teacher I find the love of poetry is better fed with choices, much like the genres in fiction.

The Japanese poetry in this last book has been extended to look at haibun, tanka as well as more of the haiku, and I look at a beautiful style called cherita.

I have taken liberties in places and have also tried to stick with the more traditional styles at other times. I will attempt to explain a little about the forms but in all sincerity, it will be a brief introduction only. I am new to this and a great believer that knowledge comes with experience, and this is an on-going process.

What I can say is there is delicacy in the way expressions, and words are presented in Japanese poetry that fascinates me. As a novice I am experimenting, learning and experimenting some more. There is a lot of fine tuning required but I refuse to be daunted. I can't let fear of errors stop me from finding my feet.

I am fully committed to encouraging me and others in attempting new things. So, what if you don't get it right? Life is about learning, the desire to get better, the joy of doing something new and different. Only by trying do we have a chance to succeed. I have done the same with my novels, experimented, tried things, read, studied and then gone back and tried again. How else can I improve? How else can anyone improve?

I hope you like my attempts and I am most happy to have your comments on any of my work. I struggle between the traditional and the modern; it is a fine balance. Input gives me perspective, so I welcome it with open mind.

Now for a little background on the newer forms I am introducing in this book. The first style is the tanka. The tanka (short song) expresses feelings and thoughts and unlike the haiku, may use figurative expressions such as a metaphor or simile. The form is less rigid than the haiku. It allows the imagination to help the poet express feelings, addressing such themes as natural beauty, love, the impermanence of life, the activities of the common people and separation.

Tanka consists of 3 lines that discuss the topic problem and then there is a shift or a comment relating back. These two lines run on. The general pattern is a 5/7/5/7/7 syllable count, but this can be modified to suit the poet's intention.

The haibun, a form that enchants me, is a short narrative with a haiku or tanka to add dimension to the previous piece. It may record a scene, or a special moment in a highly descriptive and objective manner, or may be fictional, and possibly even dream-like. The accompanying haiku or tanka may either have a direct or a more subtle relationship with the written piece. Sometimes the barely hinted gist can be enough. The clever, unique and quite beautiful way to present a thought, or idea is so appealing, as is the discipline in ensuring the prose is not an explanation of the chosen verse.

There are also other different things we can do with this form, from compacting the prose down to a small word count, anywhere between 20-to-180 words, to adding more than the one haiku or tanka, or adding both tanka and haiku. This can act as a climax or epiphany to what came before. The juxtaposition of prose and verse is important. For example, the prose should add to the depth with which we experience the verse: the verse should add meaning to the prose.

Lastly, I look at the cherita, a new discovery and one I love already. Cherita is the Malay word for a story, or tale, and is fitting for this beautifully concise creator of images. It consists of a single line stanza verse, followed by a two-line stanza, and finishes with a three-line stanza, and can be written solo or with up to three partners. This shape can be inverted and is presented, centred and untitled, with line lengths at the discretion of the poet.

You can see why I am drawn to these styles. They offer an incredible challenge to someone with an addiction to words.

Welcome to Emotions in Existence

Barbara Strickland

2019

Eruption, Evolution and Existence

Words, thoughts, buried deep.

Battle grounds as I sleep.

Eruption into volcanic ash,

The lava flow, a master's lash.

Let it go, the anger kills.

Break open the peace-filled pills.

Evolution is a flowering plant.

Rain and sun, the eternal chant.

Don't think because the poem rhymes,

that this is the place for happy times.

Existence means to walk a path.

Be aware there is an aftermath.

Eruption, let it all roll out,

an explosion of fiery doubt.

Evolution, let it take a ride,

appreciating that you tried.

Existence now takes up the tale

and lets you know it's fine to fail.

Playing with Words

I wanted an opportunity to experiment with styles and shapes, to create something based on what I know but with a twist. So in among free verse, there is a shape poem, some sonnets, poems that rhyme and poems that don't. It is more the exploration of topics in different ways that took my fancy.

A Love Sonnet or Two, my way

First Love

I don't know what it was I saw.

I don't know what it was I felt.

But that night I began to thaw

and slowly the snow began to melt.

Chocolate orbs and hair like silk

caught my heart, and with melodious voice

he read me poetry of a romantic ilk

and took away my right of choice.

I wanted to believe in a fairy tale ending,

to sigh and coo, to kiss and caress.

I wanted a love that by-passed mending.

I wanted love without all the mess.

Two weeks of paradise came and went soulfully fast.

A lifetime to regret, something not meant to last.

Love and Sin

I look up with surprise,

the blonde hair unexpected.

So was the green of his eyes,

a boon of nature perfected.

His glorious soul called to mine.

I felt the tentacles of love begin,

the strength ruled by a power divine

yet I knew the truth as simple sin.

Inside my heart I knew it could not be.

I understood that heaven had a cost.

But the heart often doesn't see,

so, I was unprepared for the frost.

The cold when love cannot survive

questions the reason to be alive.

Real Love

On love I have sat and pondered hard,

lacking faith and trust enough to recognise

the truth, written in the Valentine card.

It may sound sweet but lies are lies.

Is there truth in the whispered words of love?

Is there a potent passion pushing for shared abode?

Would the physical attraction give me a visceral shove?

Would I fall into waiting arms, or into fearful mode?

I hear, I see the twining of lips and emotions.

My voyeur heart feels the soft courtly caresses.

Couples walk past me flagrantly flaunting devotions

and yet with doubts my unsettled mind obsesses.

Love may luminate lust and be syntax clever

but I fail to see the existence of forever.

Love thrice

Smoothness of skin and fleck of gold in his hair.

Long stretch of legs and strength of baby arms.

Far too easy to learn to care

and fall for his considerable charms.

So much love cannot be repeated

until dark hair and a warming glow

proves your thoughts can be defeated

and emotions rise and continue to flow.

Now you feel safe to avow

there is nothing more you can feel

and then you find you will allow

a small butterfly, your fate to seal.

Thrice in a lifetime inside my heart,

they lay assured they have a part.

A love sonnet to the Master

When we think of sonnets, we think of Shakespeare. When we think of plays or the English language, we think of Shakespeare, and so we should. There is so much we owe to his clever manipulation of language so I thought it would be fun to play with some of the expressions we associate with him, expressions that might surprise you.

*Knock, Knock! Who's there? Suddenly I am **in a pickle**.*

*Should I **fight fire with fire**?*

***Come what may** doesn't work for the fickle,*

*and **dead as a doornail** is considered dire.*

*Are you **faint hearted** enough to leave?*

*Are you strong enough to **break the ice**?*

*Do you **wear your heart on your sleeve**?*

*Do you chance the **love is blind** dice?*

In this wild goose chase, the world is my oyster.

*The game is up on your **heart of gold**.*

*I will fight your **green-eyed monster**,*

*With **fair play, foul play** bold.*

For goodness sake, don't vanish into thin air

*To be a **laughingstock** is more than I can bear.*

I wander and I wonder

(not quite a sonnet but with thanks to Wordsworth and his love for dancing daffodils for the inspiration)

I wander aimlessly content,

admire clouds that wave to me.

I wonder without real intent

and just enjoy what I see.

Spotting then, the golden bloom

I readily let go of everyday doom.

It's not that I watch reality fade,

but rather that nature's gift

under trees that generously shade

provides a much-needed lift.

The scented fragrance gives me aim

as I walk along the way I came.

If we look with our hearts,

and are willing to see the truth inside

we can join the necessary parts.

Perceive the world, let it confide

the secret delights on offer free

available to you and me.

I'd love to have the world surround

and cushion my lonely soul.

The beauty is there all around

providing the air to make us whole.

I wander slowly and breathe with grace.

I smile, accept the sunshine on my face.

A Melody of Verse Devices

Poetry

P: patterns made with words

O: optimising language

E: emotional expressions

T: thoughts and ideas shared

R: reaping the rewards of story telling

Y: yearning for more

Poets

P: piecing together language

O: opening to ideas and thoughts

E: enabling the deeply hidden

T: teaching terrible truths

S: saving our sanity

The Poetic Triangle

words

put together

telling a small story

entertaining the waiting crowds

hoping to forge a captive connection with the seated

growing daily to encompass the revolving and constantly evolving world

forbidding the withholding or wilting of whispered waiting words we all wish we wielded

Inversion of the Poetic Triangle

constant careful complex choosing of the cunning callous communication commodity

strange struggle to display the same syntaxial alphabetical addiction

obsessive compulsion to master the symmetry of semantics

eager entertainer of the ever-waiting crowd

tale telling demands

unity of words

narrative

More than a Metaphoric Phrase

Writing, the creating of images

in words to represent

our secret thoughts and

hidden desires.

Life is stories in seething settings of

things floating, developing, and waiting.

The story is an amoebic, embryonic battle

to exist.

Condensed senses,

lighting up pages,

lighting up minds,

lighting up worlds

with their poetic devices.

The word is a magical wand delivering dreams of alliteration.

The word is an ethereal drop of softly sifted snow creating illusions.

The words wiggle, watch, whisper wickedly like mischievous children.

Bang, clash, boom, thump and bump, an onomatopoeic jump

and words claw, determined fingers at our throats forcing recognition

that the noise words make, are a metaphoric phrase to fear.

Self-destruction: a narrative

Orientation begins.

What: a life?

Where: does it matter?

When: soon.

Why: no-one to listen.

How: whatever presents itself.

Sequence of Events follows.

This way.

That way.

No way.

Too many, too hard, confusion.

Climax.

The push against the door.

The fight to complete.

The agony to receive.

The desire to succeed.

All of it coming together,

all of it falling apart, and the task

misunderstood and becomes mundane.

The climax was not the petite mort.

The climax was a series of simple sentences.

They made no sense.

Conclusion: I don't know.

Conclusion: I have nowhere to go.

Resolution: Wake up tomorrow and try again.

An Ode to Words

You are my fascination.

You are the earth,

solid and grounding.

You are the sky,

an insubstantially cloud adrift.

You are music,

a rhythmically loud sounding.

And you are melody

creating words to gift.

You are the mind

determinedly in charge.

You are language and speech,

a wielder of loud voices

in an obscene world of expression.

United harmonic travellers,

messengers on whispery wings,

reader and writer advocator,

of communication compression.

Let's go Freestyle

Habits

Undeveloped unfilled needs

acquire excuses to gratify.

Selfishness allows the easy feeds,

and excuses give cause to satisfy.

What then is sired becomes the undesired.

Ongoing, overtaking common sense

and continued confusion our recompense.

Break the habit, break the rules.

Be a rebel and desert the fools.

Standing out from the crowd should be allowed.

Pick it up today.

Don't wait another day.

Speak softer, voices low.

Be kind, let goodness flow.

Good habits can develop

or bad habits will envelop.

Depressed differences

Did you know

there are differences

in the word depressed

and the word depressed?

Not possible you say.

But possible, I reply straight away.

Although, I hesitantly add,

it may not make sense

and it may make you feel, well,

intellectually dense.

One is the chemical imbalance

of genetic warfare, fast flowing and vicious.

And the other an over preaching

of mind and psyche, a battleground

of pushing down hard

on a button you touch

and depress

because something controls you,

and the cloying claws claim.

Power has different names.

Power likes to indulge mind games.

Think about it.

Can you leave the button alone?

I can't, not while the people around me

are not listening.

CT Scan

Don't move!

Arms still.

Body rigid.

Eyes closed.

You know it was the same

when we played the marriage game.

No contact of the heart.

Bodies together but far apart.

Don't move!

You'll ruin the image.

Arms still.

Body rigid.

Eyes closed.

Just silently lie there,

your soul cold and bare.

300

It's a marriage bed,

even when the love is dead.

Don't move!

We're not quite finished.

Arms still.

Body rigid.

Eyes closed.

It's the only way

to find the source.

The only chance to say

we are way off course.

Don't move!

Make the effort

if you can

to lie with

arms still.

Body rigid.

Eyes closed.

This is just a CT scan.

The Forgetful Ones

In the middle of the night

You answer the call.

You care, you share.

It's only fair.

In the middle of life

you answer the needs.

You care, you share

yet the cupboard is screaming bare.

Now at the end of life

you need their help.

All that care you chose to share

is useless when there is no-one there.

You didn't ask,

and so, they failed the task.

Wait a minute, you forcibly say.

You taught them how to play!

They should already know,

a fancy coffin won't steal the show,

and neither will the tears, in violent flow.

Do they really believe,

do their minds truly not conceive?

It's not enough to know how to grieve,

not when they let their loved ones leave.

It's a fortunate fact

that forgiveness, a generous fact

was given steadily,

was given readily

was an irrevocable pact

long before the final act.

If not, then the closure of the lid

would be the worst thing the left behind ever did,

bringing forth memories that slid

into the void of regret,

destroying all power to forget.

Love needs a face

long before the final act.

Love needs an established place

to seal the family pact.

Love needs the spoken,

needs much more than the token.

On the edge

On the edge

On the ledge

A broken pledge

A sharp incline

A cutting line

An unexploded mine.

The hurt is cruel,

a burning toxic fuel

with heart and mind in duel.

How can they be so blind,

not notice how unkind

and how fragile the gentle mind?

But then you recall,

your choice to take the fall

because you were never one to enthral.

The price is high.

You are skin and bone.

No heart to bleed, no soul to sigh

In the darkness of alone.

Accepting the Reality

I reach for colours

of weaving waving white

for the sake of wounded warriors.

I wait for the setting of the sun

and pray for the ones still standing

hoping we will remember them.

Soldiers at arms

in eerie bloodied battlefields

of everyday struggles

still end in penetrating pain

no-one sees, that no-one notices.

The fight is fought inside the mind

and brutally battered cells

suffer spiteful torturous touches

in sickly spinning silence

of brain confinement.

We can't speak up, and

afraid to make real sounds

everything is mumbled.

Messages are stuffed in a bottle

and doomed to float to nowhere.

This is not the normal war.

This one is insidious,

an internal struggle

resulting in a deep, dark

and depraved bitterness.

This is a moratorium,

a sixties sit-in protest.

The reality like then

shows no-one listening.

When will I learn?

Anger Management

The cork swells.

The bottle struggles.

Containment please!

Stay where you are!

The balloon gasps.

The air pushes, fills.

Reasonable size please!

Big enough is enough!

Lungs expand.

The chest rises.

Pain and air collide.

Don't, don't deflate!

I can't hold it in.

The continuation never ends.

Voice crowded, headaches.

311

Stop! The twig bends,

snaps, screams

and leaves the prison cell.

And, into the black hole I fell.

Running away

There is no excuse.

There is no reply.

There is no word to cover.

There is no angel to hover.

It's all on us.

We choose.

We lose.

We win.

We sin.

Religion cannot ease.

Entities cannot please.

Limits are just a token

and rules constantly broken.

Why this need to be destroyed,

to have the soul constantly deployed

into areas of raw skin

and constantly deafening din

of pain for the insane?

Did I rhyme enough?

Or is this a piece of fluff,

a distraction from the true

grisly, gruesome death of you,

lying there all alone.

Has it happened, or is there time?

I don't know you see.

I lost track of me.

Why do we say the things we say?

Why do some of us turn away?

I wish I had answers.

I wish I had the questions.

If I knew what to say,

I wouldn't run away,

might even have the reason to stay.

Wrong Turn

I went off track

I forgot to do.

Does this happen to you?

Did you get back?

On the track, did you?

It doesn't help if we ignore

the world, the good,

if we shut the door.

We only forget we could

do so much more.

Instead we find we roam,

giving in to the constant demand of wondering.

Cleverly not leaving home

we congratulate the intelligence of pondering.

I went off track.

It's such a long way back.

Yesterday, Today and Tomorrow

I woke, I dressed and began the day.

I spoke, I listened, I went, I did.

I found time to work and time to play.

I didn't understand how fast time slid.

I was young and thoughtless

and I think a tad mindless.

I wake, I dress, I begin my day

I speak. I listen, I go, I do.

I find time to work but not to play.

I ignore the day I have in lieu

I am busy

and a little dizzy

I will wake, I will dress, and I will begin my day.

I will speak, I will listen, I will go, and I will do

but not right now I will probably say.

Not that this will be a surprise for you.

Funny thing though while you patiently wait

I realise, it could be my death that will make me late.

Outsider

I am tired of the world in between

The place I live but am never seen.

I refer to it as the existence,

the desperate desire of persistence

that has me survive every new day

and kiss goodbye the old known way.

The more knowledge we acquire

the more the burn of vicious fire.

Testing, pushing, pricking skin

stretching until it becomes too thin.

And poor protection, from outside foes

determines a definite rise in all our woes.

I am a watcher,

and a pain catcher.

I am a truth seeker

and a soul keeper.

I belong on the inside

and I tire of being denied.

Parking the Car

Mishaps on the road to life

demand a resolution,

a place to rest, to think

but the car park is full.

And so, I beg, I plead.

I hope you will concede.

I can't afford to lose face

but my vehicle is in such a bad place.

I can't believe that You, in this equation,

have no consideration.

And now I feel like dying, as if

I am losing the battle. I desire to be gone,

to disappear, dissolve and fade into nothing

with a disorientating passion?

Wait a minute, I suddenly say,

questioning my need, to be away.

There must be somewhere to park this car

and not have to travel far.

Surely it isn't much to ask,

to allow me this smallest task.

I need time-out.

I need to live.

It's just a question of time

Until someone leaves.

Yet I can't help but think

somehow, I have missed an important link.

This discussion has two themes

if we don't look beyond what seems.

I need to recall some are happy to share.

I need to believe some do care.

The noise around me is too much.

Voices blaming, lying to themselves.

And I want to leave, surrender

just to keep the peace.

It chokes me, strangling hard

writing threats on a clean white pristine card

until suffocation calls my name.

But I pull back, I refrain.

I will not shrink to their level

and allow their monstrous revel.

I wear the marks.

I bleed the blood.

I lose my speech.

I am so alone, so afraid.

Not of you, not of those I love,

not even of those ready to shove.

I am afraid of me.

For if I can allow this to be,

and let you be the one to choose,

I will be the one to lose.

Kindly place your bullying tactics elsewhere!

This is not the Bullshit Car Park,

and I have earned the right to park this damned car.

I have a place

I have a secret,

deep and dark

about the place.

Do you know what I mean?

It's the somewhere I go

when the world turns cold

and I lose the desire to be bold.

I had to search to find it.

I fought, I struggled.

Guilt came too.

Do you know what I mean?

It's the somewhere alone

when the world breaks my heart,

and casually sets me apart.

Secrets and guilt?

Deep and dark?

Strange words to explain.

But you see, there I am alone

and lately I don't want to leave.

I prefer the world I perceive.

The Boomerang Effect

Faithful to the hand.

It threw me.

Strength in the distance.

It practised.

Smooth, satin feel.

It was made with love.

Innocuous in size.

It killed something.

A tradition of centuries.

It is only a tool.

What you aim for, you hit.

A hunter's weapon.

Remember a boomerang

always comes back.

We are our own destruction.

An Italo-Australian

I heard the word.

What does it mean?

Not commonly heard or seen.

Memories made and lives merged.

Battles fought and distances purged.

Working hard in the when and where,

Grateful for the then and there.

There was no forgetting though,

the antiquity, the artistic flow.

It was heritage, an ingrained past,

a gentle blend to ensure it would last.

You request.

You respect.

You give.

You integrate.

A migrant is a citizen in waiting,

not a question for debating.

Another land is a new history.

Unknown, it is a fresh mystery.

The joining of worlds, the united segments

are an unexpected privilege.

And loyalty leaps forward

And becomes an Italo-Australian.

Oops I messed up again
(from Emotions in Eruption)

Today I fell and

turned back time.

Pushing, battling to

move on, I tired. And,

yearned for mediocrity.

The past pulls tightly

at the subconscious mind.

It has already failed to

move on because

it knows only mediocrity.

The penalty of femaleness,

to fear the independence of

aloneness.

My heart breaking,

my will forsaking,

my body shaking

with determination,

I try to stand up.

The floor is slippery.

A change of shoes may be in order.

Oops I messed up again, again

I really don't know why

And I won't try to deny

I once again lost my way

and this time I know

it was deliberate.

I really messed up today.

I interrupted the flow

and the aftermath, proliferate.

Such a costly, deadly toll.

So, what possessed me to lose control?

I don't know what to say.

I know this can't be right.

The mistakes are escalating.

Maybe I need to pray

or remember how to fight

instead of so much procrastinating.

Oh, that evil slippery floor

that simply won't allow my shoes

a smooth transition through the door.

Foolish me thought I'd paid my dues.

What is this self-doubt?

How does it come about?

Broken mirrors and illusions

lead me to into confusion.

I know who I am, I know who I'm not.

Yet daily life shows me, I forgot.

The past plays havoc in my mind

and the future becomes hard to find.

My heart breaking, my will forsaking,

my body shaking forbids me faking.

Last time I change my footwear.

I had hope.

But today, I messed up again

and changing shoes won't help.

This time I need workers' steel capped boots.

Humanality

Ignore

the voices in your head.

Ignore

the things they have said.

Humanality

the strength to not be budged.

Humanality

evokes the evolution of the judged.

It's not that simple.

The outside world can not intrude

upon the damage done by solitude.

No-one can batter.

No-one can shatter.

No-one can destroy.

No-one can deploy

the methods of our own mind

not even those of your own kind.

It's that simple.

Open your heart.

The easiest way to start.

Release your pain

and get on the freedom train.

The Box

I live in a box.

It's small and it's bare

but the square is my drawing

so, I can't yell "unfair".

I wish I could

but I drew it for me

and made the edges too sharp

to let me be free.

It's my mind, you know,

the way I perceive.

It got in a muddle

and I forgot to believe

in angels, in heaven, in

love and in trust

and while those around fluttered

I dwindled to rust.

Some of us are strong,

some of us weak.

Some don't need others

but I am a freak.

I need water.

I need sun.

I need to be staked.

I need weeds removed.

I flourish with care.

So please,

do more than stare.

Technology

The Abyss is calling.

The sound is piercing

and the frequency

only a fraction less

painful than the

hell itself.

I know, I've been to the

deep, dark and dank,

dingy dungeon that stank.

The transmission continues

to hurt my ears,

and blur my eyes.

Adjustments are

needed to filter

sounds and sights.

The blackness beckons

dangerous to the seeker,

but reality is bleaker.

I don't know if I can resist the pull.

After all, there is comfort in nothing.

The Loner Red Rose

I first saw you

in full bloom

surrounded by admirers

yet I foreshadowed gloom.

Yours, my friend.

I saw your end.

You were a rare beauty,

a crimson jewel perched high,

full, rich, hiding a splendid core.

You shone too bright to die

but sharp blades drew blood

and stupid me cried a flood.

Why this angst I asked myself?

All things must eventually fade.

I know all things have their time.

Bruised petals no longer have homage paid.

Yet this breaks my heart,

with such lingering pain.

Did the rose sit apart?

Did others think it vain?

I thought it lonely.

Perhaps instead, it chose a place

where it could pretend importance,

by flaunting its perfect face.

Did it flaunt, did it show pride,

or was it courage from inside.

Oh well, we do have to pay a price when misunderstood.

It matters not.

We, yes us, know that we are good,

don't we?

The Circle of Life

Life is a cycle, the perfect sphere.

So why does my heart react in fear?

Have you seen The Lion King?

Yes, that cartoon thing,

that has been turned into a stage play,

and possibly even a movie, someday.

Do you wonder why I ask?

Do you think I have a connected task?

Maybe I do, maybe I don't.

Maybe I'll tell you, maybe I won't.

Seriously, what's there to discuss?

Why would I consider making a fuss?

It's the circle of life, you see,

The one that spins around me,

on its axis, trailing the sun

and certainly not having much fun.

We have forgotten the circle of life

and instead concentrate on strife.

We take and we take.

The circle falters.

The shape alters.

We take and we take.

The plants die,

the land is dry.

We take and we take.

The oceans swell,

as trees we fell.

We take and we take.

Nature watches, fears for her creatures,

sighs at the destruction of her features.

Our creatures, our features we arrogantly say

standing apart, the human way.

We have forgotten the circle of life,

concentrating instead, on causing strife.

We take and we take.

Until finally, the circle we break.

The Intellectual Lover's Game

You call my name

and I cannot refrain

from playing the game

in the lover's domain.

Quietly I remain,

waiting for cruelty to maim.

Carelessly we bandy the blame.

In fairness it is hard to contain

pride, and the need for winner fame.

But, hurt is not a prize to obtain.

It festers and becomes disdain.

Too haunting, too sad to explain.

Love is a thing to retain

yet we are intellectually lame.

We pick and fashion a daisy chain

and risk unwanted shame.

We allow the other's need to reign

and subjugate and maim.

Sometimes there will be rain.

Sometimes you fail to tame.

Sometimes love leaves a stain,

on those that ride the romance train

and those that believe in a lover's lane

where no heart will ever maim.

Is there ever preparation for the pain

that leaves you shattered and a little insane?

Why did I permit him to rattle my innocent brain?

I truly hope not all outcomes will end the same.

Falling Rain: a reflection on human nature

Nature is a mirror,

a storyteller with flair.

Unique and powerful,

allowing us to learn and share.

Do you hear the soft

sprinkle and tender trickle,

of the gentle fall of drops

against your window?

Life-giving, despite the thunder

and the lightning rumble

giving life to tiny buds

reflecting infancy and simplicity.

Do you hear the disturbance

caused as cumulonimbus,

the thunder clouds, speak with

precipitation, beseech strong winds

for kindness? Praying snowdrops

prevent the boil of temperament

into the out-of-control state

reflecting teen years and fears.

The sky explodes

and the atmosphere cries

in fright, in terror wondering

where it will end and why

this incessant punishment

by nature, hurts, has no plan.

Or is there more we don't see.

Grown up worries possibly?

Ancients believes that rain

was the semen of the sky

falling to inseminate not decimate

with the grabbing greed of old age

to maintain power and control

so fearful the rain became

a series of sewers and the sweet smell

became absorbed and locked away.

I call this the unhappy times.

Things have little rhyme, little reason

to cause gaping holes in the soul

unless we are careless,

unless we ignore nature as an educator

and then there is no other recourse

but a heavy shuddering

against the glass and windowpane.

Sunset comes calling

Below the horizon, colours

bloom into a rainbow furnace,

a flaming astronomical smorgasbord,

a fencer's feint with a well-balance sword.

The start of something new,

or the end of something old?

A spectacular and unique clarity,

or an embellishment to finality?

The sun is kissed in fond farewell.

The moon responds with a subtle caress,

with a gentle soft whisper of silver rays

to wipe the memory of cancerous days.

Nature teases with its contradictions,

toys with our intellect and imagination.

If we end with something rare and beautiful,

Then perhaps we may learn to be more dutiful.

Haiku Magic

Haiku is about capturing a moment, about finding the extraordinary in the ordinary. For me the attraction is the chance to play with the nature around us and link it to our own human nature. Do I get it right? I don't know but I love trying and have no intention of stopping the process.

Concise essences
of moments to ponder life
haiku speaking

Random Ramblings

Nature

perched bird on fence

singing soulfully sweet tunes

parched land

haunting hoot

of melody and feathers

night owl wisdom

355

a soft deception

of white surfing on the wind

soft snow blanket

splattering raindrops

flutter and kiss thirsting soil

farmer diamonds

Seasons

winter deprivation

cold hands seek fireplace warmth

window wonderland

bright beading

night sky reflections

winter textures play

with the click of held needles

the winter knitter

Australian summer

heat and sea and sand and flies

barbeque weather

Life

chiaroscuro

dark shadows mock humans on display

imagination

in the depictions of life

wall art

the tease of incense

a contrast to tinkling bells

polished timber coffin

the sound of chatter

and loneliness dissipates

local brew café

grown-ups leave

the attic-holding cradle

sentimental journey

faded images

a bleaching of history

sepia speaking

chrysalis flutters

as the world around calls time

metamorphism

absolution

crawl of the caterpillars

into butterflies

a change in routine

and the heartbeat screams terror

panic-attack

a flood of tears

the front door slamming shut

single life

Festivities

sand and summer heat

in the gift giving season

Southern Hemisphere

rosemary baked potatoes

entices table sharing

wrapping paper forgotten

garland glowing

red and green with gold glitter

hands join in celebration

fire flecks burn

fragrant chestnuts and succulent ham

gifts enough

the wave of palm leaves and religious incense

chocolate egg irony

Tales of the Unexpected

A personal note: I couldn't resist the opportunity and the challenge to include my romance series in this last book. The very fact that The Unexpected Series involves travel, and a diverse set of lovers filled me with intrigue. In Emotions in Eruption I used haiku to capture some of the wonderful places my characters visit. In this book Emotions in Existence, my last in this Emotions collection, I have indulged myself again with wonderful places but have also included haiku expressing the essence of the story of each of the six books in the series. Of course, my evil plan is to entice you to read them. Here's hoping,

Barbara Strickland

Lovers, Books and The Unexpected Series

Book 1

a physical obsession for soul-kissed lovers

the unexpected

Book 2

an unexpected passion gives second chances

late in life love

Book 3

Christmas gathering brings possibilities

connections reunite

Book 4

desires in an unexpected encounter

touching the heart

Book 5

confused attraction and unexpected guilt

summer heat

Book 6

lust

odd beginnings

mistrust becomes the unexpected

Travel and The Unexpected Series

lamb and rosemary

slow roasted lemon potatoes

Greek dining

Mykonos

night market frenzy and days bathed by green seas

cocktails at sunset kiss holiday wet lips

Santorini

Delphi oracle and olives combine with ouzo tease

Athens

Medieval architecture and natural settings

Kythira

Istanbul

spices spell traveller senses bonding Europe and Asia

magic carpet rides with Aladdin's lamp

Constantinople

Catania's elephant

witness to historical invasion

Florence

home to David and beautiful decorative doors

Sienna

Gothic charms displayed on uneven stone paths

Romanesque style and glass making traditions

Murano

Tanka Talk

A cousin to the haiku, the tanka is a Japanese five-line lyric poem. It carries an intensity in the expression of emotions. There is an implication, a suggestion, a nuance of intimacy in the message it conveys. I'll let the haiku cousin explain.

concrete images
infused with intimacy
tanka nuances

migratory birds

with multi-cultural songs

fighting to blend…

assimilation

precludes disdain of skin

voices rise and fall.

with flushed faces staring

at skin pale and cold.

their world holds attention

while silent graves call

twelve succulent grapes

greet the New Year

Spanish snippets

of fiesta and red wine lips

in the midnight traditions

yellow duly bows

to shades of brown domination

on wrinkling skin -

I watch heat bow respectfully

to the soft chill of Autumn

breaking dawn dances

to the colours that welcome

golden rays of sunshine

I move and my bones protest

shattering the mood of day

Cherita Cherishing

Cherita is the Malay word for story or tale and consists of a single stanza verse, followed by a two-line verse, and lastly finishing with a three-line verse, and can be written solo or with up to three partners. It is presented centred and untitled, with line lengths at the discretion of the poet.

The soft breeze surprises

Floats and tickles

Delicate branches dance

As scattered leaves blanket

The ground sighing in relief

A finger flicks a switch – the breathing stops

Sunlight beckons

the silent stretch of arms

The sofa announces the world of Zen

while walls proclaim elegance

and the white carpet exclaims purity

The growing plant speaks life

The flash of lights

A slow walk, head held high

in the momentary stillness of the turn

The fabric clings

without lines to mar perfection

The façade holds, the model smiles

The brown gnarled spread

is a soldier in green velvet

on guard duties in the park

Silent observer, keeper of secrets

with discreet bark masking pain

A tear stained journal entry

A civilisation of decks and masts

jostling in the regimented space

A single small boat

drifting, aimless

absorbed by the marina

The homeless man in his corner

Joy is tinged in sorrow profound

as musical notes tinkle softly, solemnly

followed by the swish of fabric

Spiritual strength in the lift of arms

and in the long silent walk

The pallbearers look straight ahead.

Clothing, lacy and delicate

filling corners of the room

A feminine shower of disarray

The bitter taste of nerves

pervades, dampening the sweet fragrance

The first date

Haibun happens

Haibun is a short narrative accompanied and highlighted by, a tanka or haiku. Titles are irrelevant. Neither the narrative nor the tanka/haiku need explain the other but together they add a deeper dimension to the unfolding tale. The need for brevity and the ability to maintain a certain poignancy is at odds and thus an artistic challenge, one I wanted to try.

The window shuddered against the incessant pounding of water. They should have left sooner. Accepting the consequences of that decision, the occupant of the bed shrank further into the soft, comforting blankets, forcing perverse eyes away from the wicked sway of air causing trees to cry in pain. Hunching into an embryonic position she covered her ears, unwilling to give reverence to a wind drunk on hurricane power.

The light flicked once; the woman uttered a prayer. The light flickered again. There would be no exodus, no escape from the relentless force of nature. She sighed, resigned herself to the growing darkness. Sometimes the solution came from waiting, from patience. The disruption of noise continued, exhausting both the human and the elements themselves, until finally a shaft of light gently touched the pane of glass. Focussed now on the beam of dawn, the woman's face contorted, her body tightened and the tiny being slid into his waiting hands.

sharply piercing pain

and the final brutal push

first cry of life

He was waiting at the second tree. To go home was out of the question, and to continue to the school bus, I had to follow that path and every day the dread would grip my heart, my limbs, and finally my soul until he stepped out from the shadows of the tall green betrayers. They were supposed to hide me, not him. I fought. I kicked and scratched but he had the power, the size and the brutality that comes from the greed to encompass, swallow power like a drink on a hot day. I often wondered why someone already so powerful would need more and at the expense of the smaller, the gentle and the meek. I wasn't the only victim but at least I did try to fight back.

I did what I always did. I gave him the copy of the homework. I gave him my lunch and I gave him the small coins for that special treat at the school canteen, on Mondays. That part hurt the most. My family was in the grip of drought, nature's cruel need to dominate. Those coins were from the heart.

green yields

to a dominant autumn

bruised petals concede

The suitcases threw me. For business trips he took a small bag with the basics, and his briefcase. My mind pinched, sharply demanding I take note, real note this time of all the little things that had been happening around me for a very long time. Naturally I refused to listen. I was the perfect wife, the perfect mother, the perfect cook, the perfect fiend …I meant friend, of course I did. Where did fiend, oh forget it, a slip of the tongue even for someone as perfect as me.

I did everything by the book - instilled in me by a harsh parenting I acknowledged - but it had created someone capable of perfecting environments. I saw it reflected in my home, in my high-achieving children and in the company I kept. I did it without fussing, I did it by employing self-control.

The suitcases niggled, inciting my fingers into loud drumming on my glass-topped table. One shiny purple nail had a small chip. I shuddered. I needed to make an appointment. Now. This very minute I would ring so that itching in my eyes could settle down, the slamming of the door be ignored like all the other things I didn't like. I would fix it later…I know I would, could…

a flood of tears

as the front door shuts

single life

Glimpses

(titles generally only grace a themed group of haibun but on an emotional level I felt this piece need a name, let me know what you think)

The runner takes the first leap

and shoes, laces tight, hit the

solidity of pavement.

There is a flinch, a moment

when the challenging entity

steps out of the zone, decides

it may not be worth it. Too

late though to reconsider

for the need to win is

ingrained and selfish.

I choose to go.

The runner is focused

and fails to notice the

passing landscape, the green

of the grass, the burst of fire

from the hibiscus buds,

the fragrant scent of the roses

and the tender purple blooms

without a name. The thrill of the

workout takes precedence over

surroundings, over the

over-worked heart.

I choose to bleed.

The runner ignores the sweat

and perhaps even relishes

the liquid heat pouring

from the exertion. It is proof

of action, of doing, of being

and justifies the ignoring

of life, of people, of

everything but the satisfaction

of indulging, of gratifying

desires. I watch and shudder

but I am not that runner and I

know that the tiny heart-shaped

flowers are violets.

I choose knowledge.

petals opening

fragrance and colour follow

the beauty of spring

nature indulges senses

and new possibilities

Mum! A text?

Seems to be the only way, these days.

Nice going.

How is everyone?

Usual. Ellie nags, the children yell, and I go play golf.

LOL

LOL? Mum, u devil. Finally mastering the lingo.

ROFL

Stop, you're killing me. So, how are u?

Fine. No. A bit under the weather and was hoping you could take me to the doctor. I made an appointment.

Today? What's wrong with your car?

Just not up to driving.

Work's pretty full on right now, and Ellie has a meeting with the big guys. Can do 2morrow though.

No problem. I'll reschedule.

Great. Well, gotta keep movin, luv ya, see ya.

Bye

Sarah dropped the mobile beside her, laying back on the pillow. Her hand automatically moved to rub her chest. It didn't help the pain, but it was something to distract herself from her fears. *They were always so busy.* She closed her eyes, hoping for a respite but a sharp stabbing sensation had her gasping. She should have spoken up but these days no-one answered the phone, no-one used voices and she didn't know how to speak up in a text. Did one do it through an emoji? Exhausted she let her lids slide shut. She'd be fine. *Really. I'm fine.*

texting on mobiles

with pretty pictures and half-spelled words

discussion killer

The Art of Listening

Modern, manicured lawns and a pool sparkling in the sun – the right image for the circumstances. Nice people lived here.

The old lady laughed, a soft, bitter sound in the night as the gates closed behind her. A gated community! How perfect! No-one in without warning. Not tonight though, not until the family had enjoyed the complex a little.

A change of geography wasn't a cure of depression but right now a fragrant aroma filled the air and the oven beckoned attention.

grey marbled bench top

and Australian pine

a jarring contrast

to the shiny patch of fluid

delicately housing death

Fingers trailed the red lounge, reached down to straighten the cushions, a gift she had given her mother. The silence held an accusing tone. Was it because every time Mama had tried to say the words, she'd shut her down? Did the room know, did it hold her as accountable as she held herself? *"I'm too busy to come now. The kids have their activities. You'll be fine."* Or at other times - *"Shush, don't be silly. I haven't got time for this kind of talk."*

The pristine perfection of the room jarred Sylvie's senses. Where was the warmth, the aromas of freshly baked bread, of a lamb roast with crisp potatoes and the cakes, the slices and the fragrance of roses she always associated with her mother? Her hand circled restlessly at her throat. Sylvie took a deep, painful breath and whispered into the air. *"I didn't mean to hurt you or ignore you. Mama, you understood that, didn't you? I was busy..."*

No hand brushed away the tears. No arms held her close. No lips butterflied their way across her forehead. Sylvie wanted to scream, to blame, to hate, to pretend none of it had happened. *How did I miss the desperation, the loneliness? I didn't hear you, Mama. I heard your words, but I didn't hear you.*

the curtain flutters

and the encased body slides through

cremation

Embryonic rips

"I promise, not much longer."

"Oh God, here it comes again. I can't do this."

"Yes, you can. Breathe. In. Out. Good girl."

Go with the pain. Don't fight, don't cry. I had done this before and had prayed it would be easier this time. My body though let me down, again. Delivering babies was not my forte. My blue-eyed angel squeezed my hand.

Births like mine attracted medical students – slow dilation and the infernal drip to speed things up until, well, things sped up. The experience was too much for the over-worked and over-tired; they left after the first five hours, my husband tagging along. *Fuck him!* Blue eyes were so much nicer. I didn't question why he stayed. I didn't care. With him I could do this. But with my all-knowing husband, I mean the man kept telling me the pain wasn't that bad, let's not go there. Ah love, blind and stupid. *Don't look at the clock. Why is there one in here?* More hours of riding the ripping brutality nature decreed as *natural* and then…

"It's a girl."

I smiled, enjoying the moment. Reality would come soon enough but for now the little bundle he'd put in my arms bound us in wonder and joy, and I liked it.

butterfly kisses

in a garden of flowers

oozing pretty words –

once a year with grateful joy

Happy Mother's Day

"Why would you do that to me in front of others, undermine me, humiliate me?"

"Oh, here we go, poor you! Whatever!"

"Deflecting won't work. Not this time. Enough, now." Diana sighed. "I listen, I love you. I give you a place to lick your wounds and still you behave like a selfish, fucking cow. You need to think about your behaviour and you certainly need to think about why you do the things you do, especially lashing out at me."

Diana stood, leaning to pat the other woman on her thirty-seven-year-old-head. "Not playing the game anymore, babe. I'm too old. Being a parent doesn't mean I have to accept shit from you, so you can feel better about yourself. Call me when you learn some manners or grow up. I don't care which comes first." Diana laughed, and mentally high-fived herself as she left the café.

baby powder sweet

and midnight feedings call –

creatures of the night

approach with stealth and cunning

and suck your blood

Boisterous voices fill the room

fuelled by the refill of wine glasses

The loner walks around anxiously

Need dictates the crowd's gathering

and suddenly the socialising is serious

The launch of a new author

Or should the last line read

The launch of the next book

You decide

Hope you have enjoyed my poetic ramblings and until we meet again, I wish you beautiful things

Barbara Strickland

2019

From the Author

If you have read this far then you have finished reading **The Emotions Anthology**, a combination of my poetry books, and I thank you most humbly. I got side-tracked with this last project but in my defence the process of writing about the way we feel, about emotions we keep hidden was too cathartic to ignore. However, the time has come to return to my romantic travellers.

I have included the beginning chapters of my novel **Unexpected Obsession, Book 1** in my **The Unexpected Series,** a stand-alone contemporary romance. **Book 2, Unexpected Passion** is also a stand-alone but with frequent visits from the lead characters in the first book. This and my psychological/paranormal thriller **The Narrow Hallway,** are still in editing stages, and welcome input. I am hopeful of a release date for both in the middle of 2020.

I am so grateful you have taken the time and spent money on something I have written. Would you please consider leaving a review? Be as honest as you wish. I learn from your words and as an Indie author I know only too well that reviews can make a difference. They mean success and financial solvency. Word of mouth is an author's best friend and a brief word and a rating at Amazon or a place of your choice (depending on where you purchase the book) would be a blessing.

Thank you,

Barbara Strickland.

I don't have a newsletter but will post news, and updates at the bottom of my posts at Amorina Rose's blog (part of my website). I encourage to subscribe as I share all sorts of things including books by other authors you may enjoy.

I also have a contact email attached to my official website: www.brstrickland.com

Feel free to contact me at: barb@brstrickland.com or follow me at:

Amorina Rose's blog at www.brstrickland.com

www.goodreads.com

Amazon.com

Facebook

Twitter

Pinterest

Instagram

BookBub

Books

Unexpected Obsession (The Unexpected Series Book 1)

Emotions in Eruptions (A poetic journey through life)

Emotions in Evolution (The poetic journey continues)

Emotions in Existence (The poetic journey never ends}

TBA

The Narrow Hallway (a psychological and paranormal thriller stand-alone)

Unexpected Passion (The Unexpected Series Book 2)

Unexpected Christmas Gathering (The Unexpected Series, Book 3)

Unexpected Desire (The Unexpected Series Book 4)

Unexpected Summer Heat (The Unexpected Series Book 5)

Unexpected Outcomes (The Unexpected Series, Book 6)

Green Mists (a science fiction stand-alone romance)

Memories of the Heart (memoirs with a twist)

Lance finds Home (a children's book)

About the author

I'm an Aussie with an Italian heritage. The warmth and beauty of both cultures has always inspired me, and I thought mixing it all together and adding a few other cultures in my books would be fun. I grew up in a multi-cultural environment with a dream to speak as many languages as possible, travel till there is no more to be seen, and own a dog and cat and have space for them both. I have a degree in teaching, three children and some amazing grandchildren and love reading, reading and more reading.

Unexpected Obsession (an extract)

The Unexpected Series Book 1

Chapter 1

The scrape of the chair on the cream tiles unnerved her. The noise was an intrusion reminding her, she was unwanted here. She sat down anyway. If Lia hadn't been internally shaking from fear, she thought, she might have laughed at the two people battling to deal with her audacity, and she might have felt a little embarrassed at her behaviour.

"What the devil are you doing here? You can't be serious!" Domenico was spitting enough fire to make a dragon proud. His height, the dark eyes intense and glaring, and the tight mouth were enough on their own to make her nervous. The quiet menace in his voice was an unwanted extra. Angelia looked searchingly at the man in front of her. The gangly sixteen-year old with the pretty-boy looks had disappeared. His place was taken by a very tall and well-built stranger. The dark close to black hair was just short of military precision. Domenico's face was close shaven. The man looked like he had stepped out of a Hollywood golden era, in his black suit (designer label of course), pristine white shirt, and bold red tie. Even the black leather shoes were immaculate.

Nothing here existed of the boy, the one her seven-year-old-self had worshipped. He had towered over her, a closed, aloof scowling giant to her smaller self. Somehow, she had gotten through the barriers to win his affection. Not once had she feared him. At twenty-eight years of age her height had caught up but not enough to stop her feeling just a little afraid of the man he had become. This time around those barriers were chillingly impregnable.

She swallowed and concentrated on the couple. They on the other hand, did not seem so different. Twenty years had only aged them. Gina looked so much like Papa that Lia felt a stab at her heart. Gina had been Papa's stepsister. Nonno had remarried after Nonna Maria died. Nonna Enza had a child, a scandal in the family because she hadn't been married and no-one knew who the father was. Papa had told Lia that Nonna Enza had been related in some fashion and hence he and Gina had looked so alike it had cemented a strong sibling relationship. Gina, Papa had told Lia, had always believed Antonio to be a surprise her parents had brought home just for her. He had been her baby, not just her little stepbrother. Funny, Lia thought as an unpleasant trickle of cold slid along her spine, how one terrible moment in the past had shattered so many relationships, so many lives.

"Are you listening? What the hell are you doing here?"

"I rang first, remember?" She met his gaze bravely, aware that flinching would give him the upper hand.

"Domenico, you told her not to come. Why is she here?" Gina clutched at her heart. Unsteady in her gait, Gina leaned against the wall as she spoke. Domenico moved swiftly. He reached his mother before she lost her balance. He growled at Angelia. It made her feel sick inside. Someone else stood there watching, a thoughtful look on his face. Recognising her Uncle Lucio, Lia braced herself for another emotional outburst. Lucio remained quiet. His head tilted in surprise, but he still managed to rein in his expression enough to puzzle her. She remembered a different man, one of quick action, not this silent bystander who seemed out of place in his own home.

"You're my family. I don't need an invitation. I have every right to be here." She threw the letter she had written to them a scarce few months ago on the table. It had been returned unopened, unread just like all the other letters her father had sent to his sister over the years. "Since there is obviously something wrong with the Italian postal service, I thought I'd deliver the letter, my letter, to you in person. Funny thing though, it was marked return to sender from right here in Catania. Strange isn't it? Never mind. I have it here now. You know the letter I mean, the one about my father's accident. The one that told you he died." She released the bit of air that she had been holding in. The sound was loud in her ears. She looked away, focusing on the apartment; determined Domenico would not rattle her. It looked familiar, spotless from floor to ceiling, and the dining table was the same, a dark rich mahogany. Uncle Lucio had made it himself, and that little bit of knowledge from so long ago gave her confidence, despite the looming presence making her heartbeat faster.

"Is this how people in Australia behave? They walk into someone's home, unannounced, and uninvited?" She turned away from staring at the older man, distracted by the younger one's harsh tone. She hid her shaking hands behind her back, glad he was a distance from her. Over near the cream leather lounge where he had placed his mother, the aura he exuded was easier to handle. The lounge, another thing she remembered. Idly she mused that good pieces were pieces you kept. So why then had her aunt been so willing to throw away a lifetime of memories of the only family she had? Surely people mattered more than things?

"I told you on the phone we knew, wasn't that enough? Your father is dead..." Domenico stopped short as his mother let out an anguished moan. His face hardened further. "I'll say this in your language

Angelia, in English so there is no misunderstanding. We don't need to know any more about him or you. Naturally we sympathise but that's as far as it goes. We aren't interested in any other letters and we aren't interested in you."

"Well, isn't that too fucking bad!" Lia muttered back, making sure he could see her mouth enunciating English words. If Domenico was fluent, and he was with that almost perfect pronunciation, then she was sure he would lip read her correctly. His mouth tightened, and she smiled, a little smug at his understanding. He was fucking with her brain. Speaking to her in English as if she was a stranger, making her feel like an outsider. *Not in this lifetime, dickhead.* "I thought my aunt," she replied, in Italian and with volume, enunciating each word carefully, "might need a sympathetic ear. After all, he was the only family she had left."

"Listen to me, little girl." Gina's snarl reverberated as pain in Lia's heart, the heart searching to find the aunt she remembered. Gina was still a pretty woman despite the lines of discord marring her forehead. Her uncoloured hair needed a trim but otherwise suited her. Some women looked good going grey and Gina was one of them. "I don't need or want you here. How I feel is my business, so get out. Go home!"

The pain at Gina's obvious lack of regard or affection changed to fear at the paleness of her aunt's face, at the veins now prominent in the forehead, shiny and slick with moisture, and at the obvious breathing difficulties. A panic attack, Lia thought. Domenico was whispering calming words, but his dark eyes were turned on Lia, fierce and narrowed. None of this was going to plan. What had she expected? In her peripheral vision she saw her uncle make a move towards Gina. He halted at the vicious look his son gave him. Lia swallowed and bit the inside of her cheek, willing herself to keep still. *God there was so much happening here!* The words pounded in Lia's head. If she moved, they would see her fear and she couldn't allow that.

The letters were supposed to explain. Over the years her Papa had written his sister about everything in their lives, good and bad. She had thought to convince her aunt to read them. She hadn't thought it through. Lia hadn't realised how fragile Gina was in body. Never a large woman, she was now a small frame of breakable bones. Lia bit down on her lip with despair at the thought that not even her brother's death could dent the bitterness and hatred emanating from Gina.

"You heard her! Get out!" Domenico's voice was a bombardment. His attention on her lip worse somehow. She stopped biting on it, perturbed by the sharp gaze. "And you," Domenico barked in Italian without turning his head to his father, "go get her medication, or has this one dazzled you with her looks the way her slut of a mother did."

His continued focus on her mouth was uncomfortable. His satisfaction at this was on his face but he had miscalculated with his words. Even if he had reason to say what he did, where Marissa was concerned, it was cruel, an unnecessary taunt. It touched a raw nerve and gave purpose and strength back to Lia.

"I'm staying even if I have to sleep on the floor." Lia stood up and walked over to where she had placed her bags. She picked up her backpack from where it rested on the ground, pulled out a plastic bag and turned to face her aunt. "This has every letter my father wrote. I am not leaving until I see you read each, and every one of them. He loved you. He needed you, not your punishment. I know your reasons were good ones. They belong in the past. It may be too late for him; it's not too late for me to do this for him. You are going to read every word and then I'll go. Mark my words, you will read them. He deserves to be remembered." Lia tilted her head, letting her expression show her determination.

"Who do you think you're dealing with?" Domenico was suddenly standing in front of her. His eyes had darkened to a black abyss holding her own, prisoner. The intimidating look, the same one he had given her on opening the door strengthened her resolve. Lia held her ground, staring straight into the void. No doubt this same scenario would be repeated. She shrugged as if she hadn't a care in the world and turned away. The relief to be away from that unyielding stare nearly buckled her knees. "You're just a rude, arrogant little bitch!" His voice was a low hiss behind her, his tone menacing, the English words cold.

"It's obvious we are related then," she replied in Italian. "Although I would think arsehole suits you much better. It's more masculine." She turned and held that last word just long enough to let him know she whole-heartedly doubted the latter. Smiling inwardly, she reflected his tirade was quite mild compared to the words he might have used in his own language. That was the beauty of the Italian language, she thought, letting herself be distanced from the scene in front of her for a moment, to recoup. Swearing and name-calling were extremely creative. His reply was a supercilious sneer, annoying Lia further. She didn't censor what came next. "Perhaps, a rude arrogant bastard is more apt? Bastard, being the operative word, I'd imagine." Her words were beneath her. The gasp from her aunt testified to just how much that was true. She deserved the terrifying anger she glimpsed in Domenico before his face smoothed over.

His body was still coiled tight. Lia felt his physical battle to relax his shoulders before giving her a dismissive look. Her own body remained tense with shame. Her retort had been nasty. This wasn't her way. She wanted to erase her words but didn't know how and backing down was not an option. Fortunately, she had an unexpected reprieve from the one other person who might also have taken offence at her words.

"Leave her alone. This is my house and I say she can stay."

"Well, of course old man, you would come to her rescue. You fucked her mother in this very home, so what now? The daughter?"

Lia cringed at the crude, spiteful way Domenico had chosen to re-direct his anger at her. Lucio stood resolute, not even a blink. Lia found it painful to watch, especially since her aunt seemed unmoved by this interchange. The skin of her face though was paler, almost grey. Not the steely hue of her thick hair, but a pasty looking imitation.

"Take your mother to her room. She needs her pills and to lie down. Keep your opinions to yourself. I repeat – this is my house." His voice was quiet, yet it had an underlying strength. Not surprisingly, Domenico did as he was asked. Lia let go of the breath she was holding. Her chest no longer restricted, she turned her eyes to Lucio.

"Thank you! I'm so sorry."

"This is a very complicated household. My son took it easy on you. Next time he won't be as pleasant." She made a rude sound and he laughed. "Believe me, he let you off lightly. He is very possessive and very protective where his mother is concerned, and he was worried about her. Me, he doesn't care too much for."

Despite the silver flecks in his hair, Lucio was still an exceptionally handsome man. The bone structure heralded antiquity. A strong jaw line and an almost perfectly, oval shaped face was reminiscent of statues of Roman gods. He was taller, too, than many

Italian men, about half a head under six feet, and had an air of confidence, at least when his son's piercing gaze wasn't aimed at him. His son, Lia suspected, never lost that arrogant tilt of eyebrows. Yes. Lucio was very good-looking. So was his son. Even more so, because whilst Domenico had that same facial structure, he also had a look of Gina in the bone structure around his eyes, eyes dark like the most decadent chocolate, with long lashes most women would envy. Her father had the same eyes and so did she. Without them she would have been a clone of Marissa, her mother.

"You're different to what I expected." Lia narrowed her gaze to focus on Lucio. The cocky self-assuredness she remembered was missing. Even as a child she had noted, his confidence in his appeal as a male, in his ability to charm.

"More charming?"

She couldn't help indulging his use of that word with a small laugh. He shrugged self-deprecatingly. Lia could see sadness in those eyes.

"Age softens and changes things for some. Your aunt, my wife, is a hard woman. She lost a child and did considerable damage to her leg and we both know the how and why of it, don't we?" He waited for Lia to acknowledge his words. At her nod he continued. "I think it's too late for her to change her feelings and her ways. I am telling you, so you won't be disappointed even..."

Lia waited for him to continue, realising he was mellower, more approachable as if the edge had been rubbed right off him. Back then his good looks and surety had scared her a little. "Even...?"

"Even as I am hoping you succeed. Domenico will fight you being here. Ignore him. You are welcome to stay as long as you want. I meant what I said. This is my house."

"Thank you."

"You'll be sharing a bathroom with Domenico."

Lucio's raised eyebrows made her smile. "Is he still a clean freak?"

"You're still that bright little girl, aren't you?" Lucio laughed quietly in reply. "You have a good memory, and yes he is. Everything must have a place, usually where he puts it. Don't leave a wet sink. There are paper towels to wipe the basin down. Can you cope?"

"You're enjoying this, aren't you?" She smiled wryly, pleased to see a twinkle in his eyes wiping some of the sadness away.

"It might be just what this family needs," he replied. The twinkle was replaced with a more sombre look. "Lia, Domenico is harsh and lives by rules, usually his, but he is a good person. Too strong, far too precise in expectations, yet for all that, he has never shirked family responsibility, even with me. Give him time. Now, do you want a coffee?"

She nodded again, understanding his need to shift the conversation.

"Uncle Lucio, will she be alright? She didn't look too good."

"She gets emotional and needs medication for her heart. Your aunt…your aunt is stronger than she thinks. She didn't believe you would come. Gina hates confrontations, and to be honest she has hung on to her bitterness for so long she doesn't know anything else. Seeing you is…conflicting. She loved you so much. We all did."

He turned away, heading for the kitchen. Lia frowned. Despite all she knew of the past, she found this Lucio likeable.

"Are you sure about this?"

Halting, he turned at her question. "You look shattered! Why don't you settle into your room? Stop thinking, there's plenty of time for that."

His words made her feel safe and strangely wanted. Lia walked back to her bags, picked them up and carried them to the room with a lighter heart. She would need sheets, but Lucio was already there, handing her towels and linen before disappearing. He moved gracefully, a trait she had noticed in Domenico who had prowled the room like a cat. Lia sat on the bed, wondering again what she had got herself into, because the reality was not just this room. It comprised dinner, lunch, breakfast, using the bathroom, sleeping and doing all this in a house where she wasn't wanted.

Lucio came back with coffee. He had also thoughtfully prepared a tray containing biscuits, cheese and olives. He was quiet, unobtrusive as he put the things he carried on the small bedside table. The sadness was back in his eyes.

"I've brought you a spare set of keys." Pausing he held her eyes. "They will fight you. Just ignore them and treat this as your home. Eat when we eat. Gina will feed you. It is her way and it might provide an avenue for discussion, or not." He shrugged, looking self-conscious at Lia's intent stare. "She cooks for me, washes and irons my clothes despite the fact we haven't shared much else for twenty years, and she will do the same for you and hate you just as much. She's like that."

"Why? Why are you really allowing this?

"I owe Antonio. He was a good man, one of the best. He was my friend not just my brother-in-law. The past is a heavy burden at this age. Maybe you are the key to change. I am so tired of the cold. Today for the first time I felt a little warmth. You have brought the sun."

"Solare," she whispered at his retreating back. That had been his word for her back then, teasing her that she was sunshine. She sat for a long time after he left. Dinner that evening was not pleasant, but she stayed, refusing to be baited by either mother or son.

Chapter 2

Gina would play old records on an antiquated record player as she did the housework, and sometimes she would sing. Her voice was soft and sweet and unexpected from someone who had seemingly forgotten to smile. The first morning Lia sang along was the first time she felt Gina really saw her and not her mother, not Marissa. It wasn't hard to feel emotion and put it into the singing, after a fortnight of being ignored except in the evenings when Lucio returned from work. The ignoring did have its merits though. Shivering, even now a week later, she recalled the encounter with Domenico. It had almost sent her running home.

"Don't you know to knock?"

"This is my home, not yours, remember?"

"What do you want?"

"To give you a friendly word of warning, my dear sweet little cousin."

"Step-cousin more like it, and the little bit of blood we share is about two generations removed, thank you very much. Not that it makes a difference. Either way I'm pretty sure, your family welcome would still be underwhelming." Lia had barely restrained the smirk. Her fear of starting something held her in check and only for her aunt's sake.

"I'm watching you. I'm not my father to be swayed by looks."

His gaze had moved insolently from the pale pink polished toenails and bare feet and slowly up, stopping only when he reached her mouth. She had read too many books to let her teeth bite down on her bottom lip. The temptation was strong; it was an instinctive action. He made her uneasy, and not because he made her feel unwelcome. She wasn't sure she needed or wanted to know the reason. It was enough she understood it was his intention to make her uncomfortable. His striking presence was unsettling. Looks and personality, however, could be so at odds. She remained silent but didn't look away.

"My mother has been through too much in her life. Hurt her in any fashion and I'll make you sorry in ways you can't possibly imagine. I won't let a stronza like you contaminate the air around her."

"So, you can use the Italian language when it suits you. You're the only one doing the hurting from where I sit. I don't want to hurt anyone."

"Forgive my foolish assumption. It couldn't be because your behaviour in forcing yourself on us suggests no morals or manners."

"Thanks for the little chat. I think the only stronzo here is you. It's long overdue for you to put a sock in it. I've been trying to be polite, avoid arguments, and show you I do have manners!"

His jaw tightened in disdainful and dismissive amusement. "A sock? Is this some clever Australianism you are imparting on my poor, ignorant brain?"

His tone was polite and yet it flowed with arrogance. How did he manage that? How did he manage to make her feel stupid? "Yes, I said sock. To be exact I said put a sock in it. So, it seems you are not familiar with this particular expression. I'm surprised, as I have been quite impressed at your command of English. I can only surmise you had an excellent teacher."

Domenico just lifted the one eyebrow and waited; complete distaste for her all too evident.

"How can I explain?" Lia was close to saturation point. If he wasn't making nasty comments, he acted as if she didn't exist and spoke around her. Domenico presumed and accused, and continually taunted, despite her best efforts to be friendly, to be nice and to find her way back to the warmth and affection that had existed in the past. She suspected he knew that and took pleasure in the opposite. Perhaps what she wanted was unrealistic in these early days. Right now, though, her anger was too far gone to listen to reason.

She turned in her chair and used the wheels to push away from the desk until she was closer to him. "I said, put a sock in it, right here." Lia stretched over as she spoke and grabbed his crotch and twisted. "A sock in here will ensure that everyone understands how big a dick you actually are, not have, but are. Although I need to stress, if your dick is as pathetic as your behaviour, then it too, might be an issue, a small one but an issue."

The look on his face was priceless; her enjoyment short-lived. Domenico grabbed her wrist, forcing her hand to envelop him, a 'him', or 'it' that was a little bigger and harder than she needed to know. It throbbed. She squirmed. A feeling she couldn't even think about caused her hand to flicker against him and he, it, the thing she couldn't give a name to, jerked against her fingers. For a split second she pushed against him slowly, curiously fascinated by the way it seemed to shape itself to her hand, and the way it felt, hard and soft at the same time. Common sense and reality reared, snapping her to attention. Lia tried to pull away.

"You think you are so smart! You foolish little girl! You have no idea what you're up against. Don't ever touch me again unless you're invited, or you will get so much more than you bargained for." Domenico gave her a smug look as the colour rose from her neck to the roots of her hair.

She heard herself make a small clicking sound as she struggled to prevent the grimace her face was pursuing as she felt the embarrassing warmth pervade her cheeks. Lia tried harder to tug her hand away. He just pressed it tighter against his body. She couldn't look at him. "You already seem to have the more. Feels good, doesn't it? Or at least it does to me. I guess my dick doesn't discriminate as well as I do."

Her anger spiked. Lia squeezed and twisted hard. She wanted to hurt. Lia heard the hitch in Domenico's breathing as he tightened his grip on her wrist so cruelly, she had to open her hand. He was now hurting her. But it was worth it. He had expected her to fight him but not attack again and he hadn't been ready.

She looked up in satisfaction only to have that look die under the blaze of heat in his eyes.

"Well, well, well, it seems to me you have quite a bit of your mother in you, don't you? Like playing with dicks, do we?"

"I don't know about playing, but in your case 'dick' is the point I was trying to make." She tried to pull away. He exerted even more pressure to keep her hand in place.

"What a clever play on words. Don't look so surprised. I did have very good teachers. Good enough to know you need to widen your vocabulary. You do seem to enjoy the word 'dick'. I prefer cock myself."

The flame of heat in his eyes contrasted sharply with the coldness in his voice. Keeping her hand in his grasp he moved it to brush the solid length in a sweeping motion. His use of the word cock had shocked her. The inappropriateness was distracting, and it gave him control. Instinctively her fingers spread to cover him. In reaction his cock jerked against her hand again. The feeling it stirred created an odd connection to the more intimate parts of her body.

Lia felt sick. She glared at the face sculpted in stone. Domenico let her go. She wiped her hand ruthlessly on her jeans. The stone face cracked a little with a small smug laugh before it closed off again with an indifference that made her want to hit him. Something in his gaze though, made her wary. Lia was smart enough to recognise she was in over her head.

"That was disgusting, you are disgusting!" she muttered, completely flustered and furious and not at all able to understand a situation he had turned around so easily to his advantage. How had he gained the upper hand?

"Really? I fucking loved it. Want me to return the favour? It might add a whole new dimension to our relationship."

"What a total arsehole you are!"

"Why? Because I won 'this round'? I always win. If you don't like it, leave." Nico walked out, leaving her shaken and puzzled, and dismayed at the fact that she had referred to him as Nico even if it occurred in her mind. Why that small fact bothered her the most, considering the entire situation, was far too complex to contemplate.

The sound of her aunt's voice brought her back to the present.

"Back from the land of the fairies, are we? So, did he teach you the songs?"

Words, and not just a look or semi-growl, were a decided improvement despite the tone. Lia schooled her features to hide her excitement. She looked up from her computer where she sat every morning.

"Yes. Or sometimes it would be Mama, especially when she was sick. It helped her pass the time."

"Always the old songs, he liked the old songs, especially this one. Ha! *Calabria Mia* of all things!" Gina huffed, ignoring any mention of Lia's mother.

Lia had hoped her willingness to help around the house and with the cooking had softened Gina a little, but her aunt was not an easy person to get through to. "It's what it represented. Sicily, Calabria, in the end they all were Italians who'd left their homes, left their families. They were lonely for those things. Please read his letters," Lia asked, as she did every day, not ashamed of the plea in her voice.

"So determined!" Gina huffed again and turned away.

"Yes. You owe it to your brother."

"I don't owe anybody anything. I did nothing, it was done to me, remember? I am sure you know the story; you seem to know everything." She had her back to Lia. She went quiet and then turned slowly to glance slyly at Lia. "Tell me, little girl, will you tell me about the nightmares if I do read one?"

"Why?" It took all of Lia's self-control not to react to the sudden change in conversation.

"I'm curious about you. I don't remember you as such a rude child and I wondered maybe if guilt was manifesting itself. It can't be easy to be where you are; so obviously unwanted."

Lia shut down her computer and tried hard not to let the hurt show. So, what if she wasn't the little girl adored by her aunt? There were worse things in life. Things like losing both parents. Lia stood and walked slowly forward stopping directly in front of Gina.

"You're so determined to be the wicked, hateful witch, aren't you? Here's your chance to gloat. It's true. It's all about guilt. Too bad it's not quite the way you might imagine." Lia lifted her arms to the back of her dress, unzipped it and slowly turned her body so Gina had a good view of her back. She eased the dress aside so that Gina could follow the unsightly-looking pink line around to the front of her body. She heard Gina's surprised indrawn breath and cringed a little. Lia didn't want pity. Then again, pity was an honest emotion, and Lia wasn't too proud to take whatever she could get.

"You were there? In the car? No one told us."

"Does it matter? It doesn't make my father less dead, does it, or me, any less guilty for surviving." A gasp was followed by a tangible silence. Lia used the opportunity to pull the blue fabric back up. She almost winced when soft hands took over sliding the zip.

"How?"

Lia turned and stared at her aunt, debating the wisdom of revealing so much. The details weren't pleasant. Did Gina need the reality of the accident? Would it make her more amiable, more likely to remember the little brother she once adored? What if Lia could reach both the loving aunt and her father's sister? Lia had to try, so she hoped her smile didn't reflect the bitterness she felt.

"What do you want to know?"

***

A long-time later Lia stood, left the kitchen and came back to the table to place the first letter down in front of the tear-stained face of an old woman. Lia found the letter untouched when she returned an hour later from her room. Her aunt wasn't in the apartment; Lia hadn't heard her leave. She sat down and stared at the envelope as if waiting for an answer. *There was always tomorrow and the next day. It's not like I have to get back for work. Most of it is online.* Lia was restless. It wouldn't help her win this war of nerves. If she was to be honest, she was very disappointed in everything about this trip, at least where her family were concerned.

At the beginning she had been unsure about coming. Lia had thought Papa was trying to force things. Slowly Lia had come around. Why have families if you let them fall apart? Why then did people bother having children? Families were important; they sustained you. Sometimes things happened; it was the nature of people. Lia understood things could bring pain, but families forgave. Living in bitterness wasn't the answer. Where was the Gina she remembered, the affectionate sister, the loving aunt who had wanted a little girl just like Angelia? That woman had demonstrated an amazing capacity to feel.

Lia sighed. Her aunt was right. The damage had been done to Gina, and despite her own brother's death Gina didn't know how to let go of that. Lia wanted the affection back. She needed it. Papa had been right to want this for her. Even with all the angst, a companionship had developed between them. Gina could deny it till she was blue in the face, but Lia felt it growing. She wanted to stay. She wanted a little of that first time here so many years ago, and she wanted her superhero. She laughed at herself. *Domenico was not going to be an easy conquest.*

Things were hard enough with her aunt. Lia's shoulders shrugged dismissively. *Time to be more positive.* The boy had been so annoyed with her persistence in following him around. And then, Domenico had given in. All it had taken was for the seven-year-old Lia to put her hand in his to cross the road. He had raised those dark brows and she had smiled, not at all rebuffed by his scowl. "*Have it your way then.*" She had smiled again at his answer. He proceeded to indulge her from that day despite the teasing of his friends. That boy was still there surely even if buried in the layers of the man. Lia had patience, and she reminded herself she was a strategic planner.

Her aunt was the key to harmony. Another way to break down the barriers between them, a simpler way, might also ease the boredom of the wait. Lia needed to do some shopping for the project spinning around in her head.

***

The pattern she had chosen was simple but interesting, to encourage interaction. Pinning the squares together to make rows was a slow procedure, as the seams had to be exact. It had the desired outcome. Too strong-willed to ask questions, by the end of the week Gina had stopped resisting the lure of brightly coloured fabric and joined Lia at the table, quietly observing, never uttering a word and never picking up the letter that waited there every day.

The battle of wills was currently experiencing a gentle lull, spoiled only when Domenico came home for lunch. *If looks could kill* Lia would have shrivelled up weeks ago. This morning was different. Last night Gina had come in and soothed her when she had dreamt of the accident, and then waited until Lia had fallen asleep again. Now, Gina had picked up the pieces of material to touch them, the dressmaker in her unable to stop the need. When Gina had replaced the pieces on the table, Lia swallowed, almost afraid to breathe, as the rustle of paper was heard. She continued sewing and didn't look up once until her aunt put the letter down and silently shuffled away.

Lia picked it up and took it to her room and placed it in the plastic bag with the others. She took another one out before returning the bag to the dresser drawer. Neither woman had spoken about the previous night, yet something had changed. Tomorrow, the second letter would be on the table waiting for Gina, just as the next time the memories woke Lia, a hand would be there to chase away the darkness. *I won't make more of this than it is*, Lia kept telling herself.

***

Gina had read a letter a day now for over a week. She had also become quite vocal about the quilt Lia was creating. No other more normal conversation occurred yet the feeling of companionship continued to flourish. This morning they had baked. Later they had enjoyed the cake with coffee before setting up the sewing machine. When the phone rang, and Gina pointedly looked at Lia, she struggled not to roll her eyes at her aunt. Domenico always rang at this time.

"Pronto"

"Where's my mother?" The voice was curt, dismissive and distinctly annoyed. Lia thought of it as his trifecta tone, three winning ways to piss off Lia. She wondered what he would think of that little piece of Australianism. *There go my good intentions*. Gina would get her performance.

"Well hello to you too and thanks for asking, and yes I am well. What can I do for you?" Any conversation they had was always conducted in English. He was determined to make her feel distanced from the family, from the whole country. Lia found it amusing.

"Leave Italy but put my mother on the phone first."

Lia held the phone towards Gina.

"Tell him I'm busy and he can talk to you." Lia bit the inside of her cheek at her aunt's little game.

"She can't talk right now. Can I take a message?" Lia smiled, knowing exactly how irate he'd be at Lia's saccharine sweet tone, and his mother's behaviour. Lia and Nico both knew Gina received some sort of perverse pleasure from their confrontations even if conducted in a foreign language. Neither one though was prepared to back off. The result as usual was an unpleasant conversation with Domenico.

"I'll tell her," Lia said very politely. "Please do enjoy the rest of your day."

"Why, have you packed your bags?"

"Go fuck yourself."

"Such beautiful manners. You know, as a matter of fact, I was just about to follow that suggestion, but not on my own."

"You're a pig." With those words she slammed the phone down. She didn't miss the glimpse of humour on the normally dour face before her aunt swiftly looked away. "He's not coming home for lunch and won't be home tonight either."

"Probably Francesca again!" Gina puffed her displeasure.

It hadn't taken Lia long to learn Francesca was not liked. Having met her briefly, Lia understood perfectly. Francesca was a beautiful, egotistical bitch.

"Intelligent enough when she can get past herself. Too bad that doesn't happen often. My Nico should know better, even if her father is an important man..." Gina stopped, Lia surmised, on realising she was actually making conversation.

"They deserve each other. They're both arrogant arseholes!" Lia looked up suddenly, realising she spoken out loud. The pleasant atmosphere had just evaporated. Lia could see it reflected in the distortion of features on Gina's face.

"Because I read the letters you think you have rights now, to criticise my son and his choice of partner?"

"No, I'm sorry. I didn't mean to say anything."

"Yes, you did. You don't like my son. I'll admit he isn't very nice to you. Coming here with an agenda negated winning a popularity contest, especially since no thought was given to whom you may hurt or impose on, correct?" Gina didn't wait for a reply. "He may be difficult at times. Don't pull that face. He is my son so you, you need to keep your mouth shut. I don't care what he says to you or about you, but I do care what you say *about* him. Not to him but about him, so be very careful, Angelia, very careful."

"That isn't fair Aunt Gina. He is so..."

"Don't!"

"But..."

"I said, don't! Now let me finish reading and then another coffee and you can tell me more about Sydney."

Lia knew she would lose the little ground she had gained if she protested. She continued working in silence while her aunt went back to the letter. *There was always tomorrow. Si, domani!* Lia sighed. She seemed to be repeating the tomorrow phrase constantly, almost as often as she sighed these days. Her determination was faltering. Domenico had that effect. She kept looking for the hero of years ago and instead kept slamming up against the sharp, hard planes of a man who left the bathroom spotless and smelling expensive, exclusive and so excluding where she was concerned.

She understood he upset her equilibrium with his refusal to accept her back into the family fold. Their constant bickering shrouded something cavernous. At times an insidious element celebrated his rejection. Lia thought of it as an unexpected and complicated puzzle piece. She kept her eyes on the fabric in her hands.

***

"Fuck!" Domenico slammed the phone down on his desk in his office on the other side of the city. Something about her grated in a way he couldn't ignore. She had just walked in like she owned the place, stirring up emotions best forgotten. As if, he thought, his mother hadn't been hurt enough already with the events of the past, they now had a living reminder. In every movement, every look, the way she held her head he saw Marissa come to life, except for the eyes. Marissa's had been a sea green and her hair a touch lighter. Even so, the resemblance was uncanny and all of it pissed him off.

However, Lia's mouth annoyed him the most. The things she came out with, the language despite the innocence of that perfect face. Those little comments about his being a mamma's boy because he still lived at home were wearing thin. Lia pronounced it *mama*, an Australian idiosyncrasy that further grated on his nerves. Although he had to admit, he did incite her at every opportunity; a perverse entertainment. Domenico enjoyed making her miserable, especially since he couldn't forget the way she had stood up to him that day. A part of him had applauded her recklessness. At the same time, he wanted to squash her like a fly. She had actually touched his dick. He had never felt such anger or such a heated response. He still didn't know how he managed to stay in control of both his temper and his body. Her defiance had aroused him, had unleashed a heat he had not thought possible. It stilled burned. *That one moment when she had leaned into his rigid cock, her hand shaping...fuck her*. Why couldn't she take the hints and go back to Australia? He gave them out often enough.

Of course, the old man rushed in to defend her at every opportunity. He was eating the attention up. Who knew what went on in his mind, fawning all over her and her sweet little ways? Why was his mother being so quiet about it all? After the initial outbursts she hadn't said much at all.

He adored his mother. She'd always made him feel safe, and powerful. Not once had she complained when he needed his room a certain way, his things arranged in a certain order.

"Mamma, they have to go back exactly like this."

His father on the other hand...Nico knew the old man resented finding himself having to marry Gina. He could accept those feelings. They had certain logic. Being made to take on a wife and child for propriety couldn't have been easy. That Lucio couldn't accept Domenico's inability to fit the image in Lucio's mind of what a *son* should be was unforgivable. Now Lia had brought the whole situation to the forefront again, just by existing. His whole routine at home was thrown out.

"I don't get it." He paced around the room as he spoke and then came back to stop directly in front of his mother. "Has she become your little pet?"

"Domenico, Nico, that's not exactly a kind way to refer to the girl," she replied, not hiding her amusement at his rant.

"Well, now you're reading the letters, letting her play with your sewing machine and having cosy little meetings at the kitchen table. What the hell Ma?"

"She entertains me. She is such a determined little thing and she has some right on her side."

"What's the matter Ma? And don't shake that head at me!"

"She makes me feel lonely and confused but..."

"That's it, she has to go."

"No, you don't understand. What I mean is, she is making me see how narrow my life is and..."

"I'm not enough? Do I make it too much with my ways?"

"Nico, I enjoy doing things for you. You know that."

"No, I ask too much. I demand too much! The bitch is right. I should have my own place."

"Nico, stop! I'll admit you can be challenging," she had said with that wide smile and her eyes radiating love and warmth. "It's hard to explain, but she fills a void. In some ways she isn't so different to you, you know. She likes things clean and tidy, and she helps me willingly. I like it...I..."

"It's an act, this being so helpful. Come on, Ma. She has an agenda, a twisted one that justifies forcing herself on us."

"No, it's her. Can you let me talk?" He had nodded, if unwillingly and she had continued. "She is a sharer, of her heart and maybe a little of her soul, she has...I can't explain but she brings the sun. Solare, you father would say when she was little. Don't pout, my son. It's not like we have to admit any of this to her."

"No, she looks too much like Marissa not to have some of her nature. I don't want her here, and if she hurts you in any way...."

"You and I, Nico, have never needed anybody else. Maybe that's not right. We do need others. Leave her alone. I'm not asking you to be nice to her."

"I love you Mamma, so whatever makes you happy. You need to know I don't like it. I don't like her!"

"You did once."

"She was a child then, sweet, not this bitch with letter issues."

"Domenico, he was my brother. He was my family. Leave her alone, for me."

"Fuck!" he growled back in the present. He turned to face the woman in his office.

"Did you lock the door after Ivana left? Good girl," he said, tracing a finger from her cheek to the full red lips when she nodded. He inserted his finger and she was quick to suck on it. His cock jerked in response. "And what else did you do?" In reply Francesca dangled a black lace thong. He took it and tossed it to the floor. Tangling his hands in the back of her long thick hair, he pushed her face down towards his desk. Still holding her hair, he halted so she was just hovering, a breath away from the solid timber. "Do you see all my files, my pens, how nicely they are laid out?" He pulled on her hair and she nodded.

"Good, now remember no matter what I don't want any disruption to my desk. I have work to do later."

With those words he pushed her head down so her forehead was on the surface of the desk. He placed her hands flat above her head over the files he was working on. "Now don't move" he ordered. He hitched up her skirt, shoving his knee between her legs, pushing her thighs apart without any finesse. She whimpered and thrust her behind higher. Presumptuous bitch, he thought, tugging her hair cruelly. Indulging her wasn't a hardship on the odd occasion it suited him. Today, foreplay wasn't going to happen. She wouldn't even murmur in protest, just as she never murmured when he refused to kiss her. Francesca never knew when and what he would decide to do; it kept her eager. He initiated. She followed. He tugged her hair harder. She whimpered again, widening her stance and lifting the smooth tanned skin in a way that made it only too obvious what she wanted, what she always wanted. Her bottom was so tight. Her slit glistened. He pushed her dress up higher. She groaned, and he grinned to himself.

"Do you want my cock here?" he said, thrusting two fingers into her slickness. She moaned but shook her head. He taunted her some more before unzipping his pants. Nico let her go to sheath himself, impatient to be done. He thrust his fingers back inside her and then used the moisture on his fingers around the opening of her anus. Her whole body trembled, and his cock leaped, responding to her excitement. One long finger was replaced by two.

She panted, she moaned. She whimpered like a baby. He gave her more. He felt her muscles coiling in anticipation and reached for the little bottle on his desk. Generous with the lubrication didn't mean he gave her warning. Instead he grabbed her hips and thrust deeply. Francesca arched and cried out in pain, the kind of pain she loved.

"Yes, yes. More. Give me more."

"Do you want me to stop?" he asked harshly, his voice roughened by desire. "Answer me."

"God no," she screeched, shoving against him, impatient as always.

"Then don't tell me how I should fuck you." He pulled out and walked around to the front of the desk. She stayed perfectly still under his glare, watching as he moved his hand over his long, hard length. She salivated, licked her lips but remained quiet. He waited, staring and stroking continuously. She didn't make a sound. He walked back behind her and slid into cock heaven. A low groan escaped him at the fit. She was so tight, so desperate to set the pace. Francesca wanted that edgy pleasure badly. Nico smiled to himself. He hadn't intended to get into a serious relationship with her. Surprisingly, they suited each other well.

Francesca's pride or ego kept her faithful. She might like her sex specific and rough, but she wasn't a bed hopper. She felt herself above that. Francesca was a snob whose need to protect her reputation was at odds with her greedy, sexual and often perverse personality. If she wanted to look down on others, he didn't care. He cared that she was fastidious. In public, she used that cultured voice and well-dressed body to advantage. Her intelligence and her ability to act as a hostess were above par. It amused him to know her father was grooming her to take over the family business in the sincere belief his daughter only shit gold nuggets. Francesca ensured her father kept thinking that way. Her sense of superiority wouldn't allow anything less.

The slap of his balls against her flesh was both delicious and painful. It brought him back to the current situation. Nico had work waiting for his attention. He needed to speed things up. Nico reached for her breast, pulling on the piercing so that she bucked against him. She screamed. Her breathing, wild and ragged, egged him on so he allowed it. He relished his control of her orgasms. Increasing his thrusts to pounding, he used his fingers to mimic his actions in her weeping slit. Nico knew just what she liked. She screamed again, and he let go. *Fuck, it felt good.*

He wasted no time pulling out of her, removed the condom, tied it up and put it into one of the small bags he kept for that purpose. He watched her, noting the smile on her face as she put on her panties. Francesca wasn't at all bothered by the coldness of his withdrawal. It excited her. She saw it as an appetiser for next time. As much as was possible they were happy together in a neat little package. Functioning for him depended on a controlled environment.

He walked to the bathroom and washed his hands, smelling his fingers to ensure no remnant remained of Francesca's essence. He washed them again and looked up in the mirror as he rinsed. *That mouth, that delicious annoying mouth with those full lips that pouted so delightfully at his jibes*, he said to his image in the oval mirror, *was going to get her into so much trouble. She had far too much to say for herself.* He shook himself in annoyance as he realised exactly who he was thinking about. It wasn't Francesca.

Amazon.com

Unexpected Passion (an extract)
The Unexpected Series Book 2 (cover still needs refining)

Book 2, Unexpected Passion will centre on Alexia and Ricardo. These two strong-willed characters have more in common with each other than either one would suspect. Secrets will be revealed, and passions will surprise them both.

Alexia (Lexi to her friends and family), the heroine of the second book has a Greek background and is Lia's Godmother. Lia is the female lead in the first book of the series, Unexpected Obsession. Although I have designed the series so that each book stands alone the books do link. I wanted the people in my novels to be a family of sorts, and because in Australia we are very much multi-cultural country, I also wanted my characters to reflect this.

Lia organises a trip for Alexia that covers Italy, Greece and Turkey. Without giving spoilers our Lexi will spend time with Lia whilst in Italy. We don't exist in isolation and I thought it nice if we could continue learning more about Lia and Nico as the years progressed. This will weave through Alexia's and Ricardo romance but make no mistake this is most definitely their love story. Please read on.

Author's note: This is still very much a raw extract and will need editing. I hope you like this enough to come back for more when I publish it early in 2020. Feel free to give me feedback on this at my email address above.

Chapter 1

Alexia Georgiou was annoyed. Too many people had time on their hands and were using it to interfere in her life. Take her friend Fran, her supposedly best friend, had just spent a full two hours lecturing Alexia on packing, the packing for her trip, not Fran's trip, but hers. Fran didn't have a bee in her bonnet, she had wasps that flapped around criticising every item Alexia had put in her suitcase. The cow had pulled everything out, tossing them all over the room. *Seriously*, Alexia thought to herself, *it was her holiday and she wanted to be comfortable. Screw Fran, screw her niece Julie and screw just about everyone else she knew.*

Lexi walked past the mirror in her lounge room, determined to ignore the hair comment as well. She got three steps past it before she stopped and turned around. It needed a cut again, and yes, she conceded to her alter ego's smug reflection, with a scowl, a colour wouldn't go astray either. *Damn it. Why won't they let me lead my own life? Why does everyone assume I need fixing? If they had kept their traps shut, I wouldn't be double guessing myself.* The person in the mirror had bags under her eyes and was carrying about six kilos more than needed, so didn't answer. *Oh! Shut up! Ten kilos, then! Are you happy now?* Alexia scowled at the reflection, furious that she couldn't lie to herself. She had a week before she took off, so a hair appointment doable if she organised herself. It might be the easy compromise to keep the busy bodies happy.

She blew out a frustrated breath because Fran had made some sense. "Fran might have had a *bit of right* on her side about the hair. The bitch!" Lexi spoke the words with a British accent and a snooty look on her face. The mirror didn't laugh. *A picture did speak a thousand words.* Lexi puffed out a whoosh of air, watching it land on the mirror as mist. Leaning in, she wiped the glass and stared at the steel grey wisps, a harsh halo against her complexion; the bits of faded colour in some of the strands long past renewable. The grey washed out the pale blue of her eyes completely, and her eyes fringed by dark lashes were her best feature. Alexia had gone grey at nineteen years of age. There had been no explanation; overnight the muddy strands of brown had acquired a greyish tinge, and the change continued until the grey dominated.

To counteract the effect sensibly, Alexia had decided on streaks. The strands of gold and reddish copper had become a trademark, surprisingly easy to maintain, and adding a distinctive look that complemented her barely five-foot height and athletic build. Alexia had made her big breasts, small waist and nicely rounded behind work for her and had never lacked male attention, at least not till the last couple of years.

The face in the mirror had too much to say. Alexia poked her tongue at her reflection and picked up the phone. Idly she brushed her hands over the dark mahogany bookcase that sat underneath the oval mirror. Dust, she scowled again and wiped her hands on her pants. Maybe it was time she made some changes, beginning with herself. *Oh, the irony of it all!* She needed to change back to what she had been rather than change to something new.

Fuck! How did I let my nails get to this stage? It's not like I was busy dusting. She was in a rut, the worst kind – the kind where she didn't feel like doing anything. She dialled Trish's number. The woman would scream with glee, to get her hands back on Alexia's head for more than a trim. It would be like the scene from Moonstruck where Cher finally agrees to cover the grey.

Lexi hated the well-meaning conspiracy between her friends. She knew it meant she was an unappreciative bitch. She didn't care. They pissed her off because they were right. She dialled her hairdresser's number between curses. *I wonder if Trish has time to organise my nails.* Her reflection scrunched itself into a sneer. For the first time in a long time Alexia ignored her own negativity and let herself laugh. She had to; she looked like a damned maniac.

***

Two days later and halfway around the world, Lia put down the phone, smiling. Fran had come through with the measurements she needed to complete her little project. How Fran had managed to get Alexia to agree to having her wobbly bits measured, testified to Fran's determination, proof of how much Fran cared about her friend. She had concocted some story about a party Lia and Nico were hosting during the month Alexia would stay with them in Sicily, and that Lia wanted to make her a dress as a birthday present.

A plausible enough tale, Lia thought, given Lexi had decided to extend her visit and celebrate not only her own birthday, but also the possible birth of Lia's new baby before heading home. Lia smirked on two levels; Lexi would have some unexpected additions to her wardrobe and Lia and Nico would partake in a feast of delicious Greek food. Alexia Georgiou didn't cook, she created magic.

Lexi's slump into depression after her mother's death had frightened all those who loved Lexi. Although looking after Yiayia had drained her, Lexi had idolised the woman and the loss had devastated her. Yiayia, the Greek word for grandmother and a word Lia had used since a small child, had been a loveable blend of sweetness and roguishness. The dear old thing determined early on that if Lia didn't have a grandmother of her own, she would fill that role. Yiayia, with her short-bread biscuits, had filled that role for many if truth be told including Lia's best friend Laura.

That death had come a year after the death of Lia's Papa. He and Lexi had been best friends for nearly thirty years, and Lia suspected he would have been the one to best help Lexi through the trauma. From a teenager, Lia had secretly hoped Lexi, already a mother figure, would become a more permanent part of their lives. Instead the friendship held. There were time times Lia had wondered if they had all missed something, some clue. It had never made sense to her that two people so in tune had not become more.

Lia snapped back to the present, recalling the conversation, she'd just had with Fran. Lia hated being so far away from her friends even if living in Sicily agreed with her.
Fortunately, Nico was open to visiting Sydney at any stage after the baby was born. For now, the trip meant Lexi would be here soon and Lia could smother her in as much love as Lexi would allow. Smoothing the indigo fabric and calculating how much trim she would have to buy, the sound of the door opening startled her. She tightened the belt on the jade silk dressing gown and walked out of the study.

Her heart fluttered. Moisture pooled in that special place despite the clumsiness of the huge bump on the front of her body. Or maybe it was because of the bump? *Didn't pregnancy make you too tired for sex?* Then again, not many pregnant women had a husband like hers. Lia willed her face into a bland expression. *Too late*, she thought. His beautifully cut black trousers were tenting. She raised her brows at her husband. He laughed and kept walking the direct line to where she now stood.

"I've just had my shower. Stay away." He laughed again. *Damn the man in front of her.* She held that thought and a pout for at least five seconds. He lifted her onto the breakfast bar. He had a fetish about its height, calling it perfect for his use. Lots of furniture pieces in their home were perfect, according to Nico. "Why are you home so early? Our lunch date isn't for another couple of hours."

Nico's senses came alive at her fragrance. Arousal happened just by looking at her but when combined with coconut, cinnamon and chocolate it was impossible to reason with his cock. "My client cancelled, and I thought to myself, what can I do with the spare time? I can do some paperwork, or I could go home and spend quality time with my wife, especially when my Mamma is looking after our son."

"Damn it, you're going to mess me up, aren't you?"

"Well, if it's too much trouble I could read a book instead."

"What has reading a book got to do with the hands untying my robe…" Lia stopped talking when one of those beautifully shaped hands pushed her gently onto her back while the other wandered over the prominent belly. He bent and kissed his child before letting his lips follow a determined path.

"Nico." She whimpered as his tongue reached its target and licked the length of it.

"Do you want me to stop?"

She shook her head, too breathless to speak, and closed her eyes. The wicked instrument not only licked again but darted inside. He was slow, leisurely letting his mouth show her where his head had been all morning. She moaned, fighting the need to watch knowing it gave him a heady sense of power. Her lashes though had a mind of their own, lifting to enjoy the view, knowing full well any objections would be token.

Nico's raised brows confirmed he had been waiting for the eye contact. He grinned while his tongue continued it path to dissolve her insides. His actions were secondary. The evil man knew her well. Using her arms as leverage she raised herself onto her elbows. One hand wrapped itself in his soft dark hair. She dug her nails hard into his scalp knowing how much he relished it, his soft growls vibrating against her delicate skin. Her hormones were in permanent overdrive. His? God knew the answer to that one.

Lia tugged his hair to lift his face to hers. She barely touched his lips before he took over. He made her desperate at the best of times, but the taste of herself on his tongue scrambled her mind completely. Aggressively she thrust her tongue against his, letting him know she was ready for whatever he wanted.

Nico in turn wondered whether he would ever get enough of this woman who looked like an angel and turned into a flow of lava at his touch. He kissed her ferociously, letting the tongue that had been lapping at her essence mix with the clean fresh taste she offered. At that moment a part of him wanted her mouth on him, wanted to push his way in and fuck her mouth till he came. He craved that combined essence like a man starved for air. His impatient headstrong cock had other ideas. He kicked his pants away and let his hard length fill her.

It never failed to surprise her, this intense pleasure she received just having him inside of her. Their tongues continued to battle, mimicking the dance of body parts, pulsing and throbbing until her insides tightened, her slick softness demanding the steel rod melt against her. She moaned into his mouth as she fragmented, pushing him into his release. Sated he slumped over her, his head on her breast.

"You know," he said, his tone casual, his lips moving over her still covered nipple and breaking the quiet. "I can't decide what the man in the apartment opposite finds the most entertaining, you in this position or me without my pants."

"What? That's not possible." She cried. He grinned, and she punched at his chest, mouthing an obscenity in response to his teasing.

"What a terrible mouth you have at times. Just as well you can make better use of it at other times! You do realise he is too far across the way to see us."

"Would it bother you if he could see us?" The look he gave her made her smile. "You are a crazy perverted man. "

"You have to admit, there's a lot worthwhile to see."

His tone sent those little shivers back into play. She watched as he slid out of her and used the dressing gown to wipe himself, and then do the same for her. She punched him again for good measure.

"Lia," he asked, suddenly losing the humour in his face and moving one hand to her throat. He applied the smallest amount of pressure.

She waited quietly. When he did that it was because he felt overwhelmed. Since he had accepted, she was having this second child, he had moments when he needed to exert control. He felt he had power over her this way, or so he thought. Lia let him believe it. Some people might not understand. They had no idea of how his mind worked. Lia did. His thumb made small circles at the base of throat. Still he said nothing. He took a breath, taking her hand with his, he used the thumb of that hand to rub lightly over her engagement ring. She wondered if he knew that his left thumb was imitating his right one.

"How did you know this was the ring I wanted you to choose?"

Careful not to react to the strange way his mind worked, she let out a small sigh at the question almost three years overdue. That meant three years of thinking about it, three long years. She smiled gently and turned to him as if he had asked a perfectly simple question. "Nico, it was a square ruby, with two small square diamonds. The symmetry was perfect, the stones were bold, and the ring combined yellow and white gold. It suited us both. Of course, it would be the one you wanted. It was perfect." She crinkled her nose at him. "I imagine Seppo would have received some very exact instructions. And, I'm not surprised he could fill them. His store was full of things that would appeal. You're his landlord, aren't you?" She raised a brow and he flushed slightly. She lifted her fingers to his cheek, and he leaned in, letting her soothe him. "Nico, I know who you are."

"Yes, you do. Why?"

She didn't answer, knowing full well he wasn't ready yet. His silence indicated his own awareness of the fact. His hand continued the small caress at her throat before lifting her off the table, his face re-arranging itself to the relaxed man who had come home early just to make love to her. She bent down to pick up his things.

"Don't. Leave them," he whispered against her ear. He inhaled her fragrance as she tightened her arms around his neck and put her cheek against his. He liked that he didn't have to explain himself.

"Did you sort out Alexia?"

"Yes, I did. I have some bits and pieces to finish she doesn't know about in time hopefully in time for you to deliver when you fly to Rome. I'm confident I can."

"Good." He kissed her as swung her into his arms carry her to their bedroom. "No reason then not to concentrate on your husband."

Chapter 2

"*Where was the sign?*" There was supposed to be, a sign somewhere and Alexia Georgiou refused to take her medication in response to the agitation knocking at her mind. Anxiety had been her enemy too long. She would not panic. *She could speak the language and she was a mature person, fifty-four years old, and surely this counted for something? That's damn right. I won't panic.* She stopped to look around her reminding herself to breathe, to stay calm. Lia's friend Annalisa had seemed very efficient in all their conversations, she reassured herself.

The airport, big, noisy and so busy disconcerted her after the smoothness of the trip. *I've got to get a grip on myself, stop this infernal shaking and I'll be fine. Oh God, I've also got to stop talking to myself out loud. Shit, starting now.* She ignored the look the woman gave her but then found herself relenting. The woman recognised a case of nerves and the look appeared genuinely sympathetic. Lexi gave a small shy smile. The smile she received in return bolstered her along with the woman's words. "Tutto á posto?"

"Si, grazie." A stranger asking her if all was well settled her nerves. Lexi turned with more determination. After all she had been to Italy before even if that had been a different time with less people crowding around. She had succumbed to superstition many years ago and thrown a coin into the Trevi Fountain, several coins, and they had

brought her back. Maybe magic existed. Lord knew she could use some.
That was the real problem, not the crowed Rome airport, but the realisation that somewhere along the line over the last few years she had run out of the energy to believe in anything. The smallest things unnerved her, overwhelmed her including this trip. Acknowledging it as a good idea, didn't make it easier to be here. She wished it did because she certainly needed to relax and enjoy life again. She needed to push the panic down and keep it from ruining every experience. Breathing deep she reminded herself that travel meant adventure, a chance to find the *fun Lexi* again.

"Signorina Georgiou?" The voice, rich in tone in the way of Italian men, had a delicious accent giving her Greek name a European class which Alexia relished. Maybe her determination to embrace good vibes would pay off. She felt tingly at the timbre of his greeting. Turning to face the voice, that view was quickly challenged. The man in front of her crushed all positive thoughts and brought Negative Nellie back to the surface.

The man had yellow-brown eyes in a tanned face, cat's eyes. *Did that make sense? Did people have yellow eyes*? He frowned. *Oh shit, did I say that aloud? Too bad!* Lexi continued her slow perusal. The man remained silent. Long dark, dirty-dark blonde hair tied back in a ponytail, greeted Lexi along with an earring in his left ear and an almighty sleeve of a tattoo, or did people call it a tattoo sleeve she wondered? It started at the wrist and climbed its way past the biceps on his right arm. The thing looked like a rose bush; a climbing rose decked in glorious pinks against a green-leafed backdrop. Lexi had to admit, it had a certain charm, could be termed beautiful not that she liked tattoos, well maybe smaller ones. Surprisingly the bevy of roses added to the aura of alpha masculinity. Those tiger eyes made sure of that. He was wearing a white T-shirt, spoiled in her opinion, by the evil glare of the black skull emblazed across the chest area. She couldn't help it. Her nose wrinkled; her lips pursed unpleasantly as she continued her perusal. The man had on very well-fitting blue jeans totally ruined by the rip on one thigh and the several smaller rips on the knee and calf of the other leg. Unfortunately for her he was also wearing a badge that identified him as Ricardo from 'Paradiso Tours".

"Fuck! You have to be kidding me!" Alexia whispered, under her breath. *It was supposed to be under her breath but judging from his reaction it may have been a teeny bit louder than that.* The polite interest he had been displaying inched up a notch. There was a sudden gleam in the golden eyes that she couldn't quite read but she knew enough to know it didn't reflect well on her. The tilt of his head announced only too well that he meant it as a superior look. Now he was the one perusing her outfit, her, Flattering was not in the vocabulary of his piercing eyes.

Ricardo, she knew instinctively, was thinking the old bag had a few problems with the way she saw the world. His eyes, expressive and narrowed, branded her as one of those people that judged the surface instead of the person underneath. She felt it and he couldn't be faulted for it. She did, him at least. Normally a pragmatic person, Lexi accepted rather than judged. The last few years tolerance had taken a beating but her reading of people had remained.

Lexi swore she could see and feel his mind working to put the thoughts together. Lexi had spent too many years in a classroom with too many varying personalities not too recognise *the look*. The conversation in his brain went like this - of course he had to be the odd one, not her in her regulation navy track pants, matching zippered jacket and tourist running shoes. Lexi could feel the distain. Hell, she could practically taste it and for once Alexia wished with all her heart, she wasn't so good at reading people.
Her honesty screamed the fault as her own.

Defensive, she had judged him. He had reacted accordingly. *Why the hell did she care, what he might be thinking anyway*? Pulling herself together and settling her features into a neutrally pleasant expression, an oxymoron she knew, Lexi offered him her hand. The grip was strong and surprisingly warm. To his credit he recognised that she had had read him and he rearranged his features into a friendlier, more welcoming look but the gleam in his eyes remained. He found her amusing.

Of course, this could also be just a conversation in her head, and he might not be thinking anything. No, Alexia knew better. This man had hidden layers despite the hippie look. *Did people still say hippie, or did 'out there' fit better?* Either way, he was too old to dress like that. *Was he even a real Italian? Weren't they all well-dressed, smooth and charming by nationality?* She dug deep into her memories of her first time in their country and she was positive it had been different.

This guy looked like he should be on a surfboard at the beach or in a rock band, not representing some fancy tour company. *To be fair, his age negated the rock band notion even if things these days were more relaxed. He had to be in his fifties. Well, that didn't bode too well, did it? Damn!* Lexi did not find the idea of being stuck on a six-week tour with a 'wanabee-young', middle-aged flowerchild instead of a professional. She'd bet a lot of money on the fact that bimbos were his favourite hobby. *What the hell?* Ricardo was trying not to let his feelings show. His amusement lessened the more those lips of hers disappeared into that fake almost-smile. This was so typical of this generation of female no matter where they came from, always so ready to judge on appearance as if she could talk. *Pazienza, Ricardo*, he told himself as he repeated his question to her again. He needed an acknowledgement about her bags. Maybe he should let her have her fill of looking, at his arm, his hair, his earing and yes, the arm again. *Ma dai, ancora con questo sguardo? Get over yourself lady!* Pointedly he looked down at her luggage and back up at her face hoping to snap her attention back to his question. "Is this all you have?"

"Yes. Yes, it is." She hated sounding rattled. His fixed gaze though unnerved her. She felt measured and found wanting. Mind you, who didn't these days? Ridiculous to start her trip in this manner, with this man she barely knew. There she went again, feeling sorry for herself. Hadn't she just made up her mind to relax?
"Good. Follow me please," he said firmly, making sure he had her attention, and kept it.

She nodded, feeling a little silly, as he grabbed the blue suitcase. He led her back to the small transit vehicle. She saw three possible couples and two elderly ladies all chatting excitedly together. "Fuck! They're all American! Geez Fran, you should have come with me. This is a nightmare," she exclaimed hearing their accented voices and bit her lip as Ricardo glanced back at her. She needed a filter big time for her mouth, or at least she needed to concentrate on thinking things in her head and not saying them out loud. But come on, nearly all the people she knew that had taken tours in Europe, had warned her about loud whining Americans, so she could be forgiven for reacting the way she did.

He, Ricardo obviously disagreed, and thought her the problem. *Shit, she was the problem. Hadn't she gone off her head at the very people who had said that? Great. She was being a real cow, a judgemental bitch. Yellow eyes thought so, and she couldn't blame him. What the hell was wrong with her?* She had agreed to all of this. Ricardo, of Paradiso Tours, had every right to raise those brows, and give her that look.

The chatting had stopped. Curious and friendly smiles came her way as she boarded. She surmised the only one to have heard her little outburst was the blonde bozo. *Lucky for me!* Lexi winced, feeling awkward enough without her mouth antagonizing people before the tour even started. She smiled back and sat down quietly fiddling with her small backpack. She didn't know whether she could do this. She wasn't ready for all these people. Alexia didn't know what was worse, her fear or the battle to keep it hidden. The golden hues had darkened to a deep brown and were staring at her in the rear-view mirror. She cringed further inside her head. Her shoulders followed suit as she realised, he didn't like her and wasn't hiding it behind a polite mask. It wasn't good business but at least he was honest.

The Narrow Hallway (an extract)

Author's note: This extract needs a great deal of editing. I hope you like this enough in its raw state to come back for more when I publish early 2020. Feel free to give me feedback on this at my email address above.

Prologue

The Speaker, a tall man, dominated the room. Resplendent in white, the colour a symbol of purity, the cloak floated around him, gleaming with a life of its own. Heavy silk and lined internally with a fabric simulating animal-fur, the formal apparel donned by all present, gave a sense of unity. Despite covered heads shrouding the faces of the stilled robotic-like forms, the slant of their bodies, was identical as they awaited the final word.

"It is decided, then? Agreed?"

The Others nodded, fearful of, but satisfied with, the outcome. Sorrow, attached every time this situation arose, kept them silent. Each time an individual became a Watcher and received their instructions, apprehension ruled. The world continued its uneven weave, and the decision to spare the suffering for The Chosen became more emotional and difficult. Both Watcher and Chosen would bind, would share an exclusive synchronicity without a foreseen outcome.

Bodies, individuality hooded and hidden in the sacred robes, bowed their heads in prayer together with The Speaker. A frozen mural, waiting patiently as the heavy fury of steps dissipated, and as the newly made Watcher left them behind, they did not flinch as he slammed the door. His anger did not rob them of hope. They had after all expected it.

Part One

The Now

The Watcher

"Will you be back soon?"

"I don't know. There's less light these days. Winter's being a real shit. You know I need the light to return. The freaking hallway is playing stupid mind games. Dark and so drab. I hate it."

"I'll miss you. I hate it here alone."

My eyes, I swear, rolled back in my head of their own volition. I couldn't control it. *For fucks sake I was going to work, not the moon! This whining had to stop!* The urge to shake her and yell abuse at her, clogged my throat. Clearing it, I turned to her and gentled my voice. "I might have to stay longer; you know I don't have a choice. I need light to re-coup my energy. I'll be back when I'm back." We went through this every time I received the call these days, and patience was a battle, my own personal anger management arena. Pulling on reserves I waited for her to say more. She always said more.

"Please don't be annoyed. Something is different, worse somehow, and I am so afraid you won't come back. What will happen to me?"

"For fuck's sake, get over this. Nothing will happen to you. Stay inside. I will come back. Don't I always come back?"

Biting viciously on her bottom lip, a nervous habit that no longer excited me, her voice lowered, softened as she spoke until I could barely hear her, not that I needed the words. They never altered.

"I can't help it. I'm afraid."

God, she had become so annoying, clinging in a way I found cloying and oppressive. A part of me felt bad. I shouldn't be so impatient, shouldn't let her get to me. A body length away, I felt her tremor as she reached for me, and wondered with a calmer part of my mind, whether the fault belonged to her crazy fears, justified, given the continued changes in the hallway, and how much could be attributed to her absurd conviction I no longer cared for her. Everything these days spelled rejection.

What was she dreaming up in that broken brain? A drop of blood fell, her top lip a victim to the clean, white teeth. Perfect teeth, perfect like all her features: the small nose, the almond-shaped brown eyes, the impossibly long lashes tracing the smooth skin of the high cheekbones. The blood continued to pool and fall as she bit harder, a bizarre sensuality as it slid to the side of her mouth in perfect pearl shapes on perfect, too pale, porcelain. When had she become so colourless, so thin, and so brittle? Last night as I fucked her, my hands had caressed hip bones, a dissolving body shape.

"Watcher, please, please don't be angry. Tonight has …is…feels…I don't know but the fear is choking me. I can't breathe. I hate her. Every time you come back a part of you is gone. She's bad for you, a vampire sucking your life force. You wouldn't need the light so much if she didn't treat you the way she does. It's getting worse and there's not enough of you left, to survive it, to survive her. "

"Stop. Stop right now. This jealousy is absurd. Your paranoia is doing my fucking head in."

"Watcher, are you angry… are you really angry with me? Or with her because you know I'm right? Something is not right, she has to go, she…"

One hand closed over the luscious mouth. I wiped the blood sitting at the corner of her lips away with my thumb as my other hand circled her throat, tightening, gripping hard enough to leave angry red marks. I sighed. My mind a war zone, anger tinged the patience I needed with this fragile being, tinged then opened its mouth, swallowed and regurgitated fury. I knew her words shrieked a truth, I knew Bella had the right to say it; after all she wore the results every time I came home, suffered the violence I brought with me, shared the toll it took on me, felt the repercussions in the harsh, cruel way I took her.

Perhaps if she was different, I would be different, things would be different, wouldn't they? When had this virulent hatred of my charge taken her over? Obsession had me hear the same thing over and over until my head was ready to split apart. Just once couldn't Bella take responsibility for herself? Maybe if she wasn't so weak…so whiny I would handle my side of things, especially my job better? Where was the woman, I met that night, the woman with so much life, an independent, sensual goddess?

Goddess, not an exaggeration. I remember thinking fortunate had finally smiled on me, and big time. I had some crazy idea she was my bonus for all the shit I had to put up with. What can I say? The girl was a stunner, not young but with the kind of beauty that transcends age, transcends everything. The club that night had been crowded, more so than usual but for me she had stood out like a, I don't know, a beacon. I know that sounds clichéd. I didn't have the words then for her and not now even with all this shit going on, driving both of us into an asylum and not the good or safe kind. I just knew if it was the last thing, I did that night I would meet her, talk to her face-to-face, and I would be the one taking her home.

She had noticed me. I could tell despite the way she ducked her head behind that cloud of curly hair that framed her face. For all her beauty she wore an air of shyness indicating uncertainty. I liked that. I liked that someone so beautiful lacked confidence. It meant she took nothing for granted. A protective streak, normally reserved for my charge, took over, softened my stance. Her lips trembled but she smiled, she fucking smiled.

"Nice tattoo," I had said smoothly, letting my fingers glide gently over the small butterfly on her shoulder. Truly it was a work of art, a black, pink and vibrant blue flutter of wings sitting on a delicate branch with tiny green leaves. I had worked my way around the room until her left shoulder, bare and with a soft golden glow enticing me, sat a small breath of distance from my lips. "Got any more?" I whispered, as my lips slid to her ear. I blew on the tiny gold stud and she shivered, blushed, and leaned closer with a sweetness, a gentleness, and delicacy, a juxtaposition to the sultry looks. My heart and cock shook hands, united in their goal to have her.

"Maybe, maybe not."

My cock twitched again, pushed against the prison bars of my zipper, as she answered my question. "Bella," I growled softly. "I am going to call you Bella. It's Italian for beautiful. Yes, Bella is the only name you will answer to from now on. Bella." I repeated the name one last time before bending and sucking on the tip of that perfect ear, my breath cool. She shivered in response, allowing me to cage her closer. I knew I had her. I went home with her that night.

Don't get me wrong! The lady wasn't an easy fuck. We clicked, gelled, talked all night and until recently hadn't spent a night apart.

Meeting her coincided with a quiet period in my employment. The early days as a couple, don't laugh at this but we were together, really together, a committed couple. Anyway, that time had been free from stress. Well, up to a point. I mean, this job and stress do go together. Called out on a regular basis back then held an ease long gone, and my Bella understood what I had to do. My Bella understood many things, trusted me without questioning motives. Her continued faith in me warmed my soul. Not once did she question the fact, I had given her the same name held by my charge, my little ward.

I know what you're thinking but no, there's nothing inappropriate here, so get anything like that out of your fucking head. Little Bella is my job, my duty. Looking after her means protecting her, guarding her against all harm. The name, Bella, is something I like but then I like the Italian language. Watchers learn to speak many languages as part of our training. Italian is my favourite.

Moving on, Bella's faith in my ability to keep my job and my home life separate floored me. I felt honoured with her trust and worked hard to ensure my duties didn't impact on our lives. We were so happy, both of us. *What changed?* I shrugged, an insincere shrug for I knew full well I feared answers. *Never bullshit a bullshitter. Fuck, I knew damn well what had changed.*

I sighed, pushed my frustrations away, and let my hand cup her cheek. We stayed this way for a small precious moment until the chill distracted me. Winter, nastier than normal, a vicious cow of a season, joined the ticking clock to remind me I had to go. Cold touched my toes, wound itself up my calves, my knees and thighs and I couldn't help the shiver, couldn't stop it as the insidious evil jumped torsos. I had to go. There were things that needed doing.

First though, reassurance had to be given. Bella spoke true, a straight to the gut true. Things were worse. A fragile wisp, she needed soft words, not lies, not truth either but words, words I could give her. My Bella had intelligence, both intellectual and emotional and my Bella needed words to give her security, strength. The shivering, mine increased. *Fuck, it was beginning. I had to go.*

"I need you to be whole. Do you understand? Whole."

"Yes, I know. Don't worry."

My hand caressed her cheek, my thumb slid across her bottom lip before I bent and sucked it gently. I let go, placing a kiss on the smooth forehead. "Be my brave girl. I promise to return as quickly as I can. I always do, don't I?"

"I'll wait right here. This is my favourite room. It's where I keep all my treasures and you are the most treasured thing I have. I'll wait for you, always."

The quiet voice, touched with tenderness, and coloured by fear, hurt my heart. I did have one despite how I behaved. My gut, already a volcano of orange, leaped to a fierce red. She nodded, the movement of her head jerky, the angles of light across her cheek bones highlighting her pallor, I felt a piercing sense of panic, flames rising from the pit of my body to my chest and throat. With it came an overwhelming urge to memorise every detail before me, every tiny pore, freckle, and hair in her possession.

My woman had become a jigsaw puzzle. I wondered if the pieces would fit when I returned. Her pieces, my pieces, the jigsaw pieces didn't fit the way they should. The puzzle was harder to solve these days, the pieces not aged; they were worn, tattered. I thought of them like vertebrae. Deterioration clawed fiercely to impinge and destroy, bringing forth a cruel crunching as each piece tried desperately to find comfort. Bone on bone could never be comfortable.

Fuck, it was cold. I don't remember it this cold. See, my Bella had messed my head and even this dark, dingy, narrow hallway I had traversed for fucking forever, today held the power to faze me. How many times had I walked this path without looking back? This time, I looked back. My emotions felt raw, torn. I feared leaving her. Bella deserved better, deserved more. The moment had arrived, the moment to face certain realities clawed at my throat sending bile into a mouth dry with tension.

Further into the long claustrophobic void I felt it, that icy slide that took over my body slowly like a silken garment tantalising me, without the pleasure that is supposed to partner it. I felt it take me over, melt into my skin and possess me. It was like the prep before the procedure, the pre-anaesthetic pill to dull the senses. *Where did I find the courage?* My job had dangers, repercussions I had managed to keep at bay. How much longer could I do that?

I was so tired these days. I wanted to give in, to let it happen, let her die, her, the other one, the woman my Bella feared so passionately. Lately, she brought doubt into all I did, all I saw, not Bella, the other one, Issa. My choices niggled at the edges of my consciousness every time Issa spoke. The power to thrust doubts aside had long left me. I could no more change my profession now than I could stop breathing. *Fuck self-doubt!* I knew my job. I heard the call. I answered. Burning eyes, red-rimmed and with the itch signifying tears I plodded on. I had to. No-one else could do this. The burning increased. The tears did not fall.

I walked and walked and walked some more, and with each step I felt my body tense, fill with the necessary blood I would need. It heated my insides me even as I continued to shiver and shake. *Are you wondering why I hadn't put on warmer clothes?* It doesn't work that way. There are perks to my employment. One of those includes the ability of my body to automatically adjust to the weather but that was under normal circumstances, my life away from the job. Unfortunately, the job itself made other demands in the way of bodily reactions. The more volatile the situation the worse the toll on my body, or our body, those of Watchers in general.

Sometimes it was cold, the kind that makes me feel brittle, breakable, kind of the same way Bella looks. The ice gets into every pore, every single angle, every piece of skin and it dissects your spirit. That cold, that ruthless, insidious, deceptive slide along my bloodstream chilling me from the inside out was the definition of cruel. And yet, I still preferred it to the heat. That bastard sears the souls and burns the spirit to nothing, not even ashes. How was that possible and why was it necessary? How many times had I pondered this same question? Why the fuck was it taking so long to get there this time?

I stumbled, reached backwards to lean against the wall. Something was wrong. Slumping, I gave in to my body's desire to soften, go limp, and slid down the wall until I found myself sitting cross-legged, breathing deeply, my head in my hands. My sadly battered brain fought a losing battle against the memories roaming in a kaleidoscope of colour, tormentingly graphic. They flashed like a power point presentation: that first briefing, going before the forum, the first encounter with the child, meeting my Bella, and the nightmare moments of in-between those days and the now. Why is it we remember the bad part so clearly? Not to say I don't remember the good, but those bad moments have talons and they cut deep.

www.ingramcontent.com/pod-product-compliance
Lightning Source LLC
Chambersburg PA
CBHW020741100426
42735CB00037B/164